THE INNER GAME
OF STRESS ·

THE INNER GAME OF STRESS

Outsmart Life's Challenges
and Fulfill Your Potential

W. TIMOTHY GALLWEY

EDWARD S. HANZELIK, M.D.

and

JOHN HORTON, M.D.

RANDOM HOUSE / NEW YORK

The *Inner Game of Stress* is a work of nonfiction.
Patient names and descriptions have been changed, however,
as have identifying details of individual histories.

As of press time, the URLs displayed in this book link or refer to
existing websites on the Internet. Random House, Inc., is not
responsible for, and should not be deemed to endorse or recommend
any website other than its own or any content available on the Internet
(including without limitation at any website, blog page, information
page) that is not created by Random House. The authors, similarly,
cannot be responsible for third-party material.

Copyright © 2009 by W. Timothy Gallwey,
Edward S. Hanzelik, M.D., and John Horton, M.D.

Illustrations copyright © 2009 by Joan Swan

Published in the United States by Random House,
an imprint of The Random House Publishing Group,
a division of Random House, Inc., New York.

RANDOM HOUSE and colophon are registered trademarks
of Random House, Inc.

ISBN 978-1-4000-6791-6
eBook ISBN 978-1-58836-895-9

Library of Congress Cataloging-in-Publication Data

Gallwey, W. Timothy.
The inner game of stress : outsmart life's challenges and fulfill your potential / W. Timothy Gallwey and Edward S. Hanzelik.
p. cm.
ISBN 978-1-4000-6791-6 (alk. paper)
1. Stress (Psychology)   2. Conduct of life.   3. Happiness.
4. Games—Psychological aspects.   I. Hanzelik, Edward S.
II. Title.
BF575.S75G35 2009
155.9'042—dc22
2009013210

Printed in the United States of America on acid-free paper

www.atrandom.com
2 4 6 8 9 7 5 3 1

First Edition

Book design by Rebecca Aidlin

Dedicated to
people worldwide
who seek
stability, calm, and wisdom
in the face of life's challenges

FOREWORD:

WHAT OUR PATIENTS TAUGHT US

By John Horton, M.D.,
and Edward Hanzelik, M.D.

As DOCTORS, WE SEE THE MEDICAL EFFECTS OF STRESS EVERY DAY. THE American Institute of Stress estimates that stress is a factor in between 75 and 90 percent of all visits to primary-care doctors. That figure does not surprise us. Although medical researchers find it difficult to measure the effects of stress, doctors know intuitively and experientially that chronic stress takes a toll mentally and physically. Even if they do not put a name on it, our patients generally know how bad stress feels, and most are aware of their own constellations of symptoms. For one, it might be headache and shoulder pain; for another, nausea, diarrhea, and abdominal distress; and for a third, heart palpitations, anxiety, and depression. For some, the effect is subtle. For others, stress is contributing to a life-threatening illness.

Most of our patients realize the stress in their lives has become a physical burden, but often they don't think they have a choice in the matter. They believe that external circumstances determine their levels of stress, and that it's inevitable given their situations. They figure they've just got to accept the stress and try to push through it. Or they feel stuck and don't see how they can change their current habits, circumstances, or emotional reactions.

When we began our medical practice, we saw how profoundly stress was affecting our patients, and we were inspired by them to find ways to have an impact on the core problem—the stress itself. We tried counseling, which began to have an effect, but we needed more than just words. Our patients expressed a need for practical tools. But what tools could we, as doctors, give them?

Usually, doctors look for medical solutions to the problems they see—pills, surgery, or various therapies. But these strategies fall short in relieving stress because they do not address why the stress system gets activated in the first place. The stress system is designed as a life-saving biological response to danger, but for chronically stressed people, the system gets activated constantly, in response to everyday challenges. Mounting scientific evidence shows that constant stress is harmful to health. We wondered how we could help our patients go through the ordinary experiences of life without repeatedly activating their stress systems.

We had been friends with Tim Gallwey for a number of years, and we admired his approach to learning and his emphasis on the innate resources of individuals. In his Inner Game series of books, Tim demonstrates how people can maintain their equilibrium in the face of external stressors. We sought out Tim and discussed the possibilities of applying the insights of the Inner Game to the age-old issues of practicing medicine.

With Tim's help we began to teach our patients the tools of the Inner Game, showing how they could be used to prevent chronic stress. The phenomenal results we've achieved over the last twelve years have moved us to write this book. In fact, after many of our stress seminars, people have looked at us with gratitude and said just that: "You should write a book about this."

We have witnessed profound improvements in acute and chronic medical and psychological problems using the Inner Game. We have discovered that something as devastating and de-structive as stress is actually within our patients' control. We have seen that stress can be prevented by the artful mastery of the Inner Game.

When it comes to preventing illness and avoiding stress, our patients showed us they wanted to play a very active part. We learned that our role as doctors had to shift. We were no longer the experts with all the facts, jotting down our prescriptions, issuing orders, and demanding complete compliance. We had to become coaches, encouraging our patients to discover their own strengths and capabilities. That's where Tim's Inner Game strategies blended so well with medical practice. Even world-class athletes have coaches. Why? Because they know the coach can support them in their learning process, can help them see things they may overlook on their own, and can inspire them to greater achievement.

The role of doctor as coach is similar—to help patients discover their own wealth of resources, to support their efforts to strengthen their health, and to inspire them to find ways to avoid the harmful effects of stress. Our patients showed us they could quickly learn to change the level of stress in their lives and improve their overall well-being. They showed us that coaching was often the most powerful help we could offer.

We realize it may seem inconceivable that people could avoid stress in the face of all of life's challenges. Yet we continue to be amazed by the vast array of resources people have within themselves to live life in just this way.

We thank our patients for what they have taught us. They have opened a door for us to discover how to fully enjoy practicing medicine. In the pages of this book, you will find Inner Game strategies, grounded in current medical understanding and in the stories of our patients, which we hope will help you to reduce your experience of stress and to achieve top form in the game of your own life.

CONTENTS

PART THREE: THE INNER GAME TOOLBOX

INTRODUCTION
THE INNER GAME AND STRESS

A WORLD-CLASS GOLFER ONCE CAME TO ME FOR COACHING. SHE TOLD me she needed help with the stress she felt when she was playing the last few holes of any competition in which she was in contention for the title. "My hands begin shaking, and I lose touch with the feel of the club," she said. Her sense of pressure was heightened because if she could win just two more tournaments, she would be a candidate for inclusion in the Golf Hall of Fame.

Since it was impossible to simulate the circumstances of her stress, I asked the golfer two simple questions:

"What is the goal of golf?"

"Why do you play?"

Her initial answers were clear and simple. "The goal of golf is to complete each round with as few strokes as possible." She continued, "Why do I play? First, I love the environment, second, I love competition, and third, I love expressing my God-given talent."

I watched her closely as she responded. "So far your hands aren't shaking," I said. No foreseeable change would threaten her playing. "Are there any other reasons you can think of for why you've dedicated yourself to the game of golf?" I asked.

She reflected for a few moments, and then exclaimed, "Yes,

there are other reasons. First, I owe something to golf. Before golf I was a nobody. Golf has made me someone. And another thing—I owe something to my loyal fans, who depend on me to be in contention in every tournament."

She paused, looked at me, and said, "Now my hands are getting shaky, aren't they?"

"Yes, they are," I agreed. As soon as she shifted from talking about her love of golf to her feelings about the judgments and expectations of others, nervousness was inevitable. She was already looking down the road, to a time when she would no longer have the loyalty of fans or her identity as a pro golfer. She possessed phenomenal skills, but her inner stress—the fear of not living up to her self-image or the image projected upon her—was causing her stress and getting in the way of her performance and enjoyment of the game.

When she began to see what was blocking her, she regained her composure and started talking about all the effort that was required to stay in top form to play professional golf. It was as if she was seriously considering if it was worth it. She decided it was. Although she didn't win the next tournament she played, she was victorious in the one after it. Her elation was clear. She literally jumped for joy, into the lake beside the eighteenth hole.

This pro golfer was struggling with a reality that faces each one of us: making the distinction between who we are and what we do. We play many roles in life—parent, spouse, golfer, executive—but the outer reality is not who we truly are. One task of the Inner Game is to make that distinction, and then to allow our selves to shine through without the impediment of concepts and expectations that are not in line with our purpose. Once we do, we can be free of stress and play at our best—be it on the golf course, on the job, or in life itself. As you read this book, you will find many examples of people who changed the habitual thinking that induced stress and was not aligned with their growth. We hope these examples will inspire you to reflect and to find your own way toward being free of stress.

ABOUT THE INNER GAME

Before going on, I should say a few words about the Inner Game. It can be said that everyone is playing an inner game, whether they recognize it or not. That means that while we are all involved in *outer* games (overcoming obstacles in the outside world to reach external goals), we are at the same time faced with *inner* obstacles, such as fear, self-doubt, frustration, pain, and distractions, which prevent us from expressing our full range of capabilities and enjoying our time to the utmost. The premise of the Inner Game—the principles, methods, and tools I offer to help people win both inner and outer games—has remained constant: Success in life relies on balanced attention to both games.

At the heart of the Inner Game methodology are three principles:

1. Nonjudgmental awareness;
2. Trust in one's own self;
3. The exercise of free and conscious choice.

I originally applied the learning methodology that sprang from these principles to sports coaching, and later used it in corporate settings. I found that people could learn to overcome their inner obstacles. Without technical instructions, they could improve any skill, unlearn unproductive mental and physical habits, and enjoy themselves in the process. Seeing this happen day after day while coaching athletes and executives gave me profound confidence that anyone could learn naturally and make the changes they wanted in their lives.

There is no question that external events can invite stress. If you're worried about being laid off from your job, which is a pretty common situation these days, that's a big stressor. The question is, can you make a distinction between your job and who you are? This ability to distinguish between self and circumstance can be learned, and the payoff is clarity and perspective that will alleviate stress and help you to reach your external goals.

Mastering your inner game allows you to go through the challenges of life without becoming sick from chronic stress. The secret lies in knowing that you have choices about how you look at external events, how you define them, how you attribute meaning to them, and how you react to them mentally and emotionally. One core belief of the Inner Game is that every person has the internal wisdom to bypass the frustrations and fears that pull them into the negative cycle of stress.

For example, while I was helping tennis players learn to improve their forehands, backhands, and serves, I was really helping them learn how to perform more effectively on the inside. Learning to *learn* was more important than hitting the ball in the court; learning to overcome fear was more important than winning any given match. Learning the art of relaxed concentration can be applied to any endeavor on or off the tennis court. Thus the lessons from sports became fundamental in life. When the inner and outer games were in sync, stress decreased, performance improved, learning happened naturally, and there was heightened enjoyment of the activity. Some athletes call it "playing in the zone." The Inner Game is about learning to play in our zone in everyday life.

Another unique value of the Inner Game model and tools is that they tap into our natural capacity to fulfill essential needs. The human gift to learn can last a lifetime. Children learn to walk, talk, and play through enjoyment and curiosity. These processes are natural and pleasant. So, too, learning to achieve balance between gearing up to face a challenge and gearing down for rest and relaxation can be simple and enjoyable. We have the natural ability to be wise and calm in the midst of the barrage of daily external struggles. In this world, such a skill is worth developing.

TEAMING UP WITH THE DOCTORS

Back in the 1970s, when I was writing *The Inner Game of Tennis*, I became friends with two remarkable medical doctors, John Horton and Edd Hanzelik. We had many conversations about our respective work, and found great compatibility in each others' thinking. John and Edd were dedicated to practicing a different kind of medicine, with a focus on treating the whole person, encouraging the individual's full participation in his or her own care, and trusting the innate healing capacity of the human body. The doctors were learning from their patients that chronic stress was the source of many illnesses. They were looking for ways to help their patients resolve stress apart from medications. The doctors found the Inner Game principles and tools remarkably relevant to their patients' needs.

When I started meeting with Edd and John about the possibility of our working together on a stress seminar, I realized that stress was a lot more serious than just being a barrier to the performance of athletes or executives. It was more closely linked to medical problems than I had previously understood. It was, in fact, an open doorway to disease—a critical factor for a large percentage of the patients that come before physicians.

As I considered working with the doctors, I recalled that on one occasion I had helped an ophthalmologist design a training program for a specific and complex kind of eye surgery. I had felt sobered by the fact that what was at stake were eyeballs, not tennis balls or egos. The same sober feeling was present as I talked to the doctors about stress. Health and quality of life were at stake. Here was an opportunity to make a difference with people that transcended performance. Accepting this challenge would come to expand my understanding of the Inner Game.

Several other facts about stress helped me decide to say yes to a collaboration with the doctors. Chronic stress, I was learning, was much more prevalent and harmful than I had realized. And it seemed to be caused largely by the way people *perceived* the events and circumstances of their lives—and not the realities themselves.

I learned that the remedies offered for chronic stress by the medical community were often medication-based, and usually failed to address the causes of stress. Other standard remedies, such as exercise, diet, and rest, while good things in themselves, again proved inadequate in addressing the cause. Finally, the doctors made me aware of the latest medical research, which supported the fundamental principles and methods used in the Inner Game, and helped me understand the possibility of accessing human abilities that lay deeper than physical or intellectual coordination.

I began to see that the Inner Game could address the perceptual causes of fear, frustration, and pain in a way that could help people learn, through an enjoyable process of self-discovery. This process was aimed not so much at getting rid of stress as it was at the more positive goal of building a dynamic inner stability, something of inherent value to all human beings, not just when they are in a state of stress.

THE PROMISE OF THE INNER GAME

The primary strategy of our stress seminars has been to help people build an inner life stable enough to be resilient in the face of the external stressors that inevitably come our way. In this book, we will offer the fruit of our discoveries and our understanding about how to achieve this stability—and with it the hope that life can be led without the harmful effects of chronic stress.

In the following pages, John, Edd, and I will take you on a journey of learning to play the Inner Game, blending my work with athletes and executives with the doctors' patients' stories and medical insights.

In Part One, we'll describe the Inner Game principles in the context of stress, and help you get a sense of your own stress level. You'll find that this understanding alone will begin to produce a change in your stress response. That's the beauty of true learning. It is not an abstract process, but creates an organic shift in the way you view the world and respond to it.

In Part Two, we'll help you identify your roots of stability. Here the focus will be not so much on the stress you're experiencing as on the innate resources you possess that will keep you an-

chored in the face of it. Or, as one of our stress seminar participants put it, "When the shit hits the fan, you don't have to hit it,
too." We'll teach the importance of establishing roots of stability
to keep you steady over the long haul, and of creating a shield to
fend off stressors in daily life.

Part Three is the Inner Game toolbox—eight practical and effective tools you can use to increase your stability and combat
daily stressors. I have been teaching these tools to athletes and executives for many years, and we employ them in our seminars. You
can pull them out when you're facing a tough challenge, or just
rely on them for daily strength. Pick and choose those that speak
to your circumstances. Knowing you have such a powerful toolbox
of support will in itself give you more confidence and inner security. You will be able to make the changes you really want to make
in your life.

We have included exercises throughout this book so you can
apply what we are saying to your own life situation. Choose how
you want to use these exercises. You could do some and mark others to come back to later. You could write your responses in a note-
book as you read the book. You could choose to just read the
exercises and reflect on them. Our hope is that you will find your
own way to best use the exercises in applying the material to your
personal experiences.

I ONCE HEARD how Tiger Woods' father coached him about how to
deal with stress while playing golf. He told Tiger it was okay to
feel any emotion on the golf course just as long as he did not hang
on to it for more than ten steps. A picture comes to mind of Tiger
Woods, strolling down the fairway to the green, cool and confident. He seems unaware of the crowd, completely settled within
his own realm of comfort, imbued with a quiet energy and concentration. It's not a question of being unaware, or of being cut off
from the crowd. It's a matter of being able to stay within his skin
and not get in his own way. We can all have that ability.

PART ONE

THE GAME OF STRESS

ONE

Who Needs Stress?

"I'm so stressed!" We hear it dozens of times a day. It's said in different ways in different languages all over the world. Here where I live in California, stress is a way of life. We worry about the fires that are eating away at our natural beauty, or the earth-quakes and floods swallowing homes. We worry about the price of gas that is choking our car-driven culture. We worry about our economic survival, layoffs, war, and health care. If you want to worry, you've come to the right century!

That we are beset by both global and everyday stressors is ob-vious to most of us. The barrage of media messages we receive is like an assault—economic collapse, home foreclosures, terrorism, wars, loss of savings, starvation, bankruptcies, natural disasters, and failing health care systems. These messages accentuate the strain we feel from ordinary stressors, such as arguments with our spouses, difficulties raising our children, getting overburdened at work, struggling to pay the bills, health concerns, and so on.

Unfortunately, stress feeds upon stress. The more stressed we are, the easier it is for the little things to upset us. Worry impairs our ability to think clearly and function productively, and that in turn stresses us out even more. In fact, we are so used to being stressed that we have come to think of it as a normal part of our lives.

Yet stress is not normal. It is an imbalance experienced in the body when the stress system is chronically activated. The factors, or stressors, can be internal or external, but one thing is clear. The stress we feel is uncomfortable, interferes with our ability to function, and is generally harmful to our physical health.

One of Edd Hanzelik's patients once declared, "I think it would be very strange to be free of stress." In fact, there can be a seductive energy to living a high-stress lifestyle. Some people even think that stress is good for you—that it motivates you and gives you a competitive edge. When I coach businesspeople, I see that attitude all the time: "You've got to be more aggressive than the competition to succeed. You've got to drive yourself. You've got to have a warrior mind-set." In our society, we even admire people who live on adrenaline, with their buzzing BlackBerrys and eighteen-hour workdays. We consider it a badge of honor if someone can get by on four or five hours of sleep a night.

We're conditioned to view stress as necessary and inevitable, but the opposite is true. Our bodies seek homeostasis—balance. That is what's natural, and that is what works. Likewise, our minds need to be in balance, not in turmoil. Priorities need to be clear, and that includes our own well-being. It's a myth that we need stress to achieve high performance. In fact, studies show that chronic stress impairs our health, leads to serious disease, and impedes successful performance.

When we do see individuals who are beset by great challenges, yet manage to keep their cool, we are impressed. While he was running for president, Barack Obama was dubbed by the media, "No Drama Obama," and his calm demeanor gave increased hope to people around the world. Another outstanding example is Nelson Mandela. After spending twenty-seven years in a prison in South Africa, he emerged to form a government with those who had jailed him. He later said about this time, "For the political prisoners, determination and wisdom overcame fear and human frailty."

We all are in some ways imprisoned by the threats around us, or by our own personal situations. For some, illness is a prison. For others, grief, poverty or family struggles become paralyzing realities. The question then becomes, how can we access our own determination and wisdom, and not be overwhelmed by helplessness and hopelessness? Just as stress breeds more stress, hope and wisdom breed stability and well-being, no matter what comes at us from the outside.

PRESSURE VS. CHALLENGE

We can begin by acknowledging our own role in creating stress. I am reminded of an interview with a relatively unknown Brazilian tennis player named Gustavo Kuerten, who went on to win the French Open three times. Reporters, amazed that he was defeating more highly ranked players, asked, "How do you handle all that pressure?" His response was, "What pressure? It's not like I handled the pressure. I didn't feel it." No one seemed to understand his response. The press kept asking, "How could you not feel pressure under these circumstances?" He said, "I had a wonderful time. I enjoyed playing these people. I enjoyed playing well. I don't get it—what is it about this pressure?"

Obviously, to the reporters, "pressure" was a reality that existed at higher levels of competition. But to Kuerten, it *wasn't* a reality. What was real to him was that he had the opportunity to compete with the best players in the world and to enjoy playing well. He was playing in a mental state that reinforced enjoyment and a high level of performance. In such a state there is little room for stress to enter.

Perhaps it should be added that Kuerten, after winning his first French Open in 1997, did not remain stress free. His growing popularity in Brazil, and the high expectations of others, did trigger for him something he perceived as pressure, and his tennis game suffered for several years. He didn't win the Open again until 2000.

This idea that we need pressure to succeed is imbedded in us from childhood. From about three years old, the pressure is on— walk faster, talk more, do better. It's a constant theme throughout our lives. It never stops. In my experience, though, it's when you stop pressuring yourself that you can be more successful. There is something innate in all of us that wants to improve. Yet when I coach executives, they have a hard time grasping that fact. The assumption of the boss is, "Unless I put the pressure on, the job won't get done." And the employees will say, "If I don't *look* like I'm pushing the limits, the boss will think I'm not working hard." This is an unproductive cycle.

It's important here to make a distinction between *pressure* and *challenge*. When I feel I have a challenge in front of me that I accept as something I want to do my best with, I generally don't get stressed, yet I can rise to the occasion. I am alert, and my abilities are accessible to me. Pressure, although we experience it on the inside, feels like something is pushing us from the outside. Living up to the expectations of others has replaced our own motivation to excel. With pressure comes fear of failure and inner conflict. With accepted challenge comes relaxed concentration, clarity of intention, and the ability to reach for one's best. Both put us in a state of aroused attention. But an accepted challenge, though it may produce tiredness at the end, does not carry with it the harmful physical and mental by-products of stress.

I once coached the sales teams of a fine East Coast consulting company. I explained to all the teams that sales performance was not the only "game" at play. The other challenges included what they learned in the process of selling and how much they enjoyed themselves. These, I suggested, were the three stable components of work: performance, learning, and enjoyment.

I recommended that for the sake of the company's success, as well as their own personal success, they try to balance these three work goals. What I did not know was that the lowest-ranking sales team took this to heart and decided that they were feeling so pressured to perform that they weren't doing very well. The team leader, determined to redress the imbalance, told them, "For the next month, I want you to go out there and enjoy yourselves and learn as much as you can about the customer and how he views our product and how he views the competitor's product." His basic balancing message was, "Be curious and enjoy."

I heard about this a month later when it turned out that this team had come from last place to first place in sales. Obviously, when the pressure was taken off of performance, the challenge to perform remained, as demonstrated by their results. What they perhaps didn't realize at the time was that the energy they had put into this non-pressured approach was the kind that could be replicated over and over, without the experience of burnout.

The three components of work are interdependent. If, in the drive toward performance, the learning component is ignored, performance will inevitably fall or level out. Likewise, if enjoyment is missing from the work equation, both learning and performance will suffer. This holds true in all human activities.

PATIENT FILE
————————

from Edd Hanzelik, M.D.

THE SEDUCTION OF STRESS

Sam, fifty-two, was a good example of a man who relied on stress, but it was killing him. With the urging of his wife and friends, he reluctantly made an appointment to visit our practice. Sam had multiple physical symptoms, including headaches, nausea, abdominal pain, occasional vomiting, and a shaky feeling inside. He dragged his feet about seeing a doctor because he was terrified of receiving a diagnosis of cancer or even a brain tumor. I put Sam through a full battery of tests and did a thorough physical examination, and did not find a single physical abnormality.

"How can I be feeling so bad and all the tests be normal?" Sam asked. When I suggested that stress could be at the root of his symptoms, he was surprised and a bit defensive. Like many hard-charging businesspeople, Sam considered stress a necessary part of his work life—something he could handle. His job providing business services to the aerospace industry was challenging, and it involved long hours and many ups and downs, but that's how he earned a living. In a sense Sam was more frightened of losing his "stress edge" than he was of the symptoms themselves. I'd heard this before. Some of our patients even describe themselves as "adrenaline junkies," and say that if you don't have a stress-related problem, it is assumed you are not working hard enough.

But the human body is not designed to deal with chronic stress. The stress system is a built-in, life-saving physiological response for emergency survival situations. It is not intended to be a permanent state. When the stress system is geared up, it creates a chemical imbalance; if homeostasis is not restored, physical, mental, emotional, and social well-being are greatly impaired.

With coaching, Sam learned that his stress didn't give him an edge at all—and that the opposite of stress is not being laid-back. It's being stable in the face of the upheavals of life and work. Over time, Sam accepted that stress was having a significantly negative impact on his ability to function. He became more open to learning how he could maintain a sense of well-being, no matter what was happening in the world around him. "I've discovered I have to say no sometimes," he acknowledged. "I've stopped attacking myself for not doing better, and I now recognize that my job doesn't make sense if I can't feel good while I'm doing it." This was a significant breakthrough for Sam, and it had a big effect on his medical situation.

We've learned through our practice that the most common type of stress—the effort to adapt to unreasonable outside pressures, while neglecting one's own needs—is often the most deadly. Such adaptation may seem inconsequential and very normal, but it is clear that it will eventually lead to depletion, which, in turn, leads to illness. That's why one of the first things we want to know about new patients is how stretched they are. It didn't surprise me that with a reduction of anxiety and stress, Sam's symptoms began to ease. Simple awareness of what is can have a more dramatic impact than most people realize. But acceptance was only the first step. Moving beyond stress requires a serious commitment, and it was up to Sam to choose whether or not he would make it.

GOT STRESS?

Before we go on, I'd like you to spend a few moments taking your stress temperature. The experience of stress is not an abstraction. This is not a book about some generic thing called stress. It's real and personal, and the way you experience your own level of stress will inform the way you approach the rest of this book. Stress is also harmful to your health, so taking your temperature will tell you if you have what we call a "stress fever," and how serious that fever is.

On a sheet of paper, answer the following questions:

1. Without thinking much about it, write down a number between zero and ten that reflects how stressed you've been feeling lately.

2. Now write down all of the possible stressors that might be contributing to that stress. Place a number between one and ten according to how much stress it is evoking in you. For example:

   - Boss imposing an unrealistic deadline. (7)
   - Fight with teenage son. (5)
   - Can't pay the electric bill. (9)
   - Elderly parent needs hospitalization. (8)
   - Time to buy a wedding gift for a friend. (3)

   Your list can be long or short. Even small things can be stressors—such as discovering you're out of milk when your kids are clamoring for their breakfast cereal. On a daily basis, all those small stressors adding up can really get to us.

3. Write down how these stressors are making you feel. What are your symptoms—physical, emotional, mental, and social? For example:

   Physical symptoms   sweaty palms, headache, stomach pain

Emotional symptoms being on the verge of tears, feeling like punching the wall

Mental symptoms foggy mind, inability to concentrate

Social symptoms Worry that you'll fail and your boss will judge you, and may even dismiss you

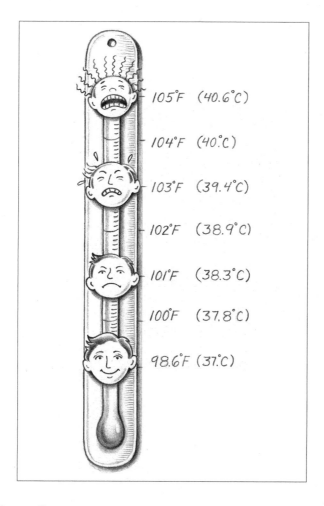

105°F (40.6°C)

104°F (40.°C)

103°F (39.4°C)

102°F (38.9°C)

101°F (38.3°C)

100°F (37.8°C)

98.6°F (37.°C)

4. After reflecting on your answers and reviewing the descriptions below, place yourself on the stress thermometer.

98.6°F (37°C) Your temperature is "normal." You feel relaxed, rested, and productive. You enjoy recreation. You take the time to reflect about what is happening to you. You're free of stress-related symptoms, physically, mentally, emotionally, and socially. You feel good.

100.0°F (37.8°C)   You have mild stress and some stress-related symptoms, such as tightness in your lower neck muscles, or indigestion. You may feel a little hyper, or slightly tired. Your stress is not greatly interfering with your enjoyment, your clarity, or your productivity.

101.0°F (38.3°C)   You have moderate stress. Your body is being affected, physically, mentally, emotionally, or socially. You feel a little more fatigued. Responsibilities are showing up as burdens that could affect your overall balance.

102.0°F (38.9°C)   You have serious stress. You're irritable, and stress is affecting you a lot. Your body and mind are showing the effects of stress. You can't think as clearly as usual. You feel moderately fatigued and burdened much of the time. You worry that one or two more burdens could topple you.

103.0°F (39.4°C)   You're approaching dangerous levels of stress. Your body and mind are seriously affected with stress-related symptoms. One more stressor and you could crack. You feel exhausted most of the time. Dealing with normal responsibilities seems especially uncomfortable. You are consciously or unconsciously looking for escapes.

104.0F (40.0°C) or greater   You're toxic with stress. You have a stress-related illness. You have many symptoms in your body and mind that you know are due to stress. You don't see how you can stop it. You're fearful of what will happen next. You're exhausted. Normal responsibilities are being seriously compromised. You need substances to cope and to sleep. One more stressor could topple you.

Normally, if you have a fever, you take it seriously. You stay home from work. You rest. If your temperature is over 101, you seek medical help. You don't say, "I'll just push through this." It's no different with a stress fever, yet many people think they can tough it out, ignore it, take substances to feel better, and adapt to it. The longer you've had a stress fever, and the more severe it is, the less likely you can shrug it off.

I hope this little exercise has made you more aware of how stress is affecting you. To overcome it, you need a strategy that is more profound than stress management. You wouldn't try to "manage" a fever, and you can't manage stress. You can, however, overcome it.

PLAYING THE INNER GAME OFFERS ANOTHER CHOICE

Most of the conversations we hear about stress are focused on getting rid of the bad stuff. People who say, "Stress is harmful," also ask, "How do I get rid of it?" But do you want your life to be about getting rid of bad things? Fighting stress, or even trying to manage it, doesn't work. You need to set a more intelligent and positive goal. The Inner Game offers a different choice—to focus on what you *do* want.

Playing the Inner Game is about building a core of stability that allows you to perform at the top of your game while avoiding the consequences of chronic stress. With this stability, you can maintain balance, clarity, awareness, and peacefulness in the face of the many unpredictable challenges life presents.

Exercise: Choose Your Stress

Look over the list of stressors you wrote down above when doing the Stress Thermometer exercise, and choose one or more to focus on as you read and perform the exercises and apply the tools in this book. Choose stressors that, when resolved, would make a meaningful difference in your life.

TWO

Our Two Selves

THE INNER GAME IS BASED ON TWO PROPOSITIONS. FIRST, THAT WE all have inner resources beyond what we realize. And second, that we get in the way of using those resources more than we would like to admit.

This realization came into focus many years ago when I was coaching tennis, and it unlocked a major mystery for me. Why was it that I and my students played so well at times, only to see our games fall back into a habitual mediocrity? In both myself and my students, I saw a continuous inner dialogue going on. While the ball was approaching, there was a barrage of self-instructional thoughts: *Bend your knees . . . get your racquet back early, meet the ball in front of you, follow through . . . Damn! You missed it . . . Watch the ball . . . Oh, this is embarrassing . . . Come on . . . Come on . . .*

Clearly, there were two "selves" on the court—the one who was actually playing tennis, and the one who was instructing, judging, and worrying. I called the one doing the talking Self 1—the invented self that was filled with concepts and expectations about right and wrong, should and shouldn't, desirable and not desirable. I called the one doing the actual playing Self 2. The problem in tennis—and, I came to see, in life—was that Self 1 was like a dime-store calculator trying to run the show, and in the process getting in the way of the performance of a billion-dollar super computer, Self 2.

Self 1 was filled with the concepts and expectations of others, and usually delivered them with the voice of a drill sergeant. He couldn't play, but, boy, did he have plenty of criticisms! The dialogue created an inner environment of stress that was ultimately destructive to the goal of hitting the ball well. The more Self 1 was engaged, the worse Self 2 performed.

From Self 1's perspective, learning a skill like playing tennis was hard. You'd have to figure out where to hold your arm, how to get into the proper ready position, and all the mechanics of the strokes. The instant self-judgment came into the mind, stress was evoked, the stroke was thrown off course, and the results suffered.

What was wrong with this picture? I started thinking about the body's natural wisdom. I like to describe it in terms of learning to walk. What would happen if we taught children to walk the way we teach people to play tennis? You can imagine the instructions: "Hold your left foot parallel to your right foot . . . lift it three inches off the ground . . . now set it down three inches to the front, while moving your body forward . . . then lift your right foot . . . watch your arms . . . they should be swinging slightly forward . . . no, not too much . . ."

It's a laughable idea. Learning to walk is not achieved with a set of instructions and positions. It's natural. Children pick themselves up, move, fall, get up, and try again. There is no self-judgment, just trial and correction. There is both simplicity and joy in this natural learning.

My aim as a tennis coach became to help people learn to play tennis ignoring the stressful interference of Self 1 and calling on their own natural abilities.

MOLLY'S STORY: WHEN SELF 1 IS IGNORED

My experience with a woman named Molly shows what is possible when Self 1 is silenced. After the publication of *The Inner Game of Tennis*, I got a call from ABC TV. They wanted to come to California and do a twenty-minute segment on the Inner Game that would be part of the well-known *Reasoner Report*. Harry Reasoner was skeptical of my claim that anyone could quickly learn to play tennis, regardless of skill or physical condition. He wanted to test the theory. The plan was to find a group of people who had never held a tennis racquet in their hands, and then see how much tennis they learned after only twenty minutes of Inner Game coaching.

Of the group that came, the producers selected a student for the televised demonstration, who from her first shots seemed the most likely *not* to succeed. Molly was a white-haired, somewhat overweight woman in her fifties, who came dressed in a Hawaiian muumuu, saying that she had done nothing physical in the last twenty years, and was sure that nothing could make her able to play tennis.

During the warm-up, Molly completely missed every ball that was hit to her. She felt understandably stressed, not wanting to be shown on television doing something she knew she was no good at. I have to admit to some stress myself, as Molly, in her muumuu, nervously holding a racquet, was to be the Inner Game's first exposure on national TV.

After giving a short talk to the group about natural learning, I asked Molly to do a simple focusing exercise. "First, I'll hit a few balls, and I want you to say the word 'bounce' the moment the ball hits the court, and 'hit' the moment the ball would hit the racquet. Don't worry about hitting the ball, just say 'hit' when you *would* hit the ball." I observed Molly carefully as she was watching the ball, and after a few moments I noticed that she was quite focused and relaxed. I saw that she was unconsciously micro moving her racquet in perfect time with the "bounce-hits." Then I asked her to go ahead and swing whenever she felt comfortable.

She missed the first shot. I encouraged her not to worry, but to just keep saying "bounce-hit" on time, and she didn't miss another ball. Not only did she not miss, but I could see her stroke developing before my eyes. It started with a simple back-and-forth motion, and within five minutes was moving in a smooth elliptical fashion that I might previously have only taught to beginners after a few months.

Next, I asked Molly simply to listen carefully to the sound of the ball on her racquet without saying "bounce-hit." When it came time for the backhand, I instructed her to just "listen on this side for a while." Which she did, while developing a better and better backhand stroke, without even knowing she was hitting "backhands." Meanwhile, I was hitting balls to her from the back of the court, increasing the challenge as I saw she was keeping her focus. I never complimented her for a good shot nor gave any indication that something was wrong with shots she didn't hit over the net.

Molly was clearly so absorbed in the process of bounce-hit that she forgot all about the three TV cameras recording her every movement. She was relaxed and having fun. And I was so focused on Molly and her learning that I forgot the cameras, too, and also lost track of time. There were only three minutes left and we hadn't started to learn the serve.

I told Molly that the serve was like a dance, and she could count the cadence of my motion. She watched me, chanting, "da, da, Da," while I hit about five serves. Then I asked her to imagine in her mind's eye herself serving, and to continue saying "da, da, Da" in time with her image of herself serving. When I saw that she was relaxed, and again her racquet was beginning to move as she counted the cadence, I asked her to go ahead and let herself hit the ball. Again she missed the first shot—but not another after. What was so amazing to me was that not only did Molly not miss a serve, but that all the fundamental elements of a good serve showed up at once. Her rhythm was natural and synchronized. There were no over-tightened muscles; she had a motion that I could only describe as truly graceful.

The twenty minutes were soon over, and the ABC producers wanted Molly to play a game with me, with her serving. We did, and the average rally lasted about ten balls. During the longest rally, I told Molly the point was going on too long and I was going to start hitting the ball harder and harder, which I did. Molly showed no signs of stress. On the contrary, she moved toward each of my balls, hitting them out in front of her with a natural authority. After about seventeen shots, she finally ran all the way across the court in her muumuu, and stretched out to hit a forehand, which struck the top of the net and fell onto my side of the court, winning the point. She leaped up in the air with spontaneous exuberance.

The film of the lesson ended with Molly hitting in slow motion one forehand and one backhand. Amazingly, her strokes were so technically sound they could have been shown to teach beginners how to stroke the tennis ball. But there was something else that was more astounding to me, and that was seeing the human qualities that were expressed in Molly's movements. There was an unwavering focus of attention and a dancelike gracefulness. But there was also a peacefulness, a quiet confidence, and an underlying joy of playing, which never seemed to break, even when her ball didn't hit its mark. Molly's Self 2 was displaying what natural learning could look like, but could never be taught. It was poetry in motion.

There are many ways to explain this beginning performance. One is that Molly focused her attention so completely in the present that there was simply no room for Self 1's stressful instructions or judgments, good or bad. Rather, Self 2, in a very childlike but adroit manner, was allowed to express the talent she didn't know she had. Another way to explain it is that Molly was in a state of relaxed concentration for the entire lesson, and the learning environment was safe enough (free of judgment) that in spite of all the reasons she might have had for being stressed, her stress system was never triggered. It was a remarkable example of Self 1 being silenced so that Self 2's inner resources could be manifested.

(If you'd like to see the Molly demonstration for yourself, it's available on YouTube and on The Inner Game website, at www .innergameofstress.com.)

STRESS AND THE UH-OH EXPERIENCE

One day, while reflecting about the relationship between Self 1 and Self 2 in tennis, I saw a cycle of reactions that I called the "uh-oh" experience. This cycle is very pertinent to many of the stress reactions we experience in everyday life.

If there is a beginning to the cycle, it's the way Self 1 puts a spin on a perceived situation. Say a tennis player is not very confident of her backhand. During a match, she sees a ball coming deep to her backhand side. Self 1 does not see a *ball*, it sees a *threat* coming right toward her weakness. This fear-based perception of the ball is enough to trigger the stress system, with all its physiological re-actions, including the freeze, flight, and fight behaviors—some-times all three in a single stroke.

Perhaps the player's initial response is to *freeze*—a moment of hesitation where there is no action at all. This is likely to be quickly followed by a *flight*, or defensive response—she backs up in hope of avoiding the inevitable mistake. Then, when there is no choice, she thinks, *I should hit this ball in front of me! Get the weight on the front foot—uh-oh, my opponent is rushing the net.* She then stabs at the ball aggressively with over-tightened muscles in an awkward *fighting* motion.

So the distortion in perception leads to a distortion in re-sponse, which inevitably leads to a distortion in results. When a player sees a "bad shot" fly off her racquet, the final step in the cycle occurs: Self 1 says, "I have a terrible backhand," confirming the distortion which led her into a self-fulfilling prophecy in the first place. The next backhand is now going to look like an even greater threat. This cycle can easily continue until it becomes a pattern, part of the way she thinks about herself as a tennis player.

One interesting thing about this cycle is that behind it all is a very capable Self 2 doing the best it can in spite of all the interference from Self 1's distortions. It is adroitly acting out the drama of perception that Self 1 is imposing on it. Even a competent player can tend to see certain shots as threats and have just enough Self 1 interference that stress is evoked, a minor distortion is introduced into the shot, and an error is made. It's just a matter of degree.

Clearly, this Uh-oh cycle can be re-created in situations that have nothing to do with tennis. Imagine the Uh-oh cycles triggered by an angry boss, a disobedient child, a nagging spouse, a difficult problem, a plunge in the stock market, another project piled onto an already full to-do list, an opposite opinion, a personal loss, or any unexpected change. All are external events that are, in effect, flying toward you, which can easily be perceived as threats and set the Uh-oh cycle in motion.

On the other hand, they might also be perceived as focused

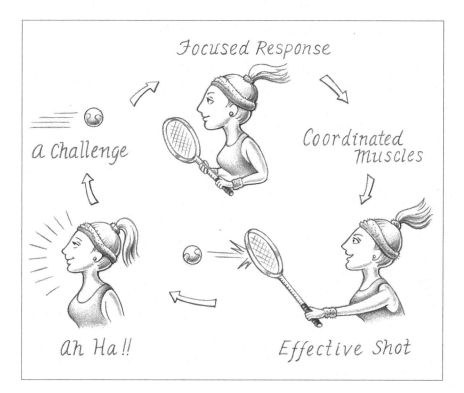

challenges that enhance concentration and inspire a creative response. Then the same cycle becomes a learning experience—an "Ah-ha!" instead of an "Uh-oh."

Exercise: Identifying Self 1 Spin

Take one of the stressful situations you identified in the Stress Thermometer exercise in Chapter One. Write down three to five examples of Self 1 spin—the inner commentary that makes this situation appear threatening.

SO, WHICH SELF AM I?

The story of David is a wonderful example of the coexistence of our two selves. David was a volunteer in an Inner Game demonstration of learning and coaching. His complaint was clear and emphatic. "I have a very defensive backhand volley," he asserted with complete certainty that he knew what he was talking about. I asked him to step up to the net and let me see for myself, thinking that he, being an intermediate player, was probably exaggerating the case. But when I saw him step back at each shot and ineffectually flail at the backhands I hit him, I said, "Yes, that has to be one of the most defensive volleys I've ever seen." David seemed relieved that his problem was seen and acknowledged by the coach. But then I said, "I can see why you don't like that stroke, but what I don't know is how you'd like to hit it." He began to explain, "Well I'd like it to be more powerful . . ."

I cut him off, saying, "No, don't tell me, show me. Show me how you'd like to hit the ball some day, and then maybe I can coach you toward that goal."

David took my request seriously, and he started to show me. The first few balls he hit out in front of him, like never before, and then he said, "No, not like that. . . . More like this." At this point he started hitting very forceful backhand volleys into the corners with a kind of fierce intensity, never leaving the mind-set that he was just trying to show me what he'd like. Soon the audience started laughing, and the "spell" was about to be broken. I said, "David, it's too bad you can't hit backhand volleys like that right now."

Instantly, David retreated to his former defensive shots. I said, "Yes, that's how you *do* hit them, but show me again how you would *like* to." As instantly as his forceful backhands had disappeared, they returned. "Like that. . . . And that. . . ." Every time he caught himself hitting his shots like he "knew" he couldn't, the old backhand would return. He went back and forth several times, like day following night.

I ended the demonstration, and David approached me with his head down. When he got to me, he stopped, looked me in the eyes, and said with a somewhat trembling voice. "So, who am I?"

His confusion was obvious. There seemed to be two people within him. Was he the person who for twenty years had "proved" to himself and others that he had a defensive volley, or was he the one that for a few minutes had shown that he could hit amazingly aggressive, powerful backhands?

"It's your choice," was all I could think to say at the time.

Clearly, David's body was capable of doing what he thought he couldn't do. Being an experienced player, he must have had a clear image in his brain of a forceful backhand volley. But in the stress mode, he didn't have access to it.

Not all demonstrations are so black and white. But in my language, Self 1 had completely convinced David that he had a very defensive backhand volley. However, Self 2 was always there, ready to come out, once the brain circuits were switched. Self 1 had never told David that he couldn't *show* me how he'd like to hit the ball. It seemed like a reasonable request. So he did. Self 1's stress circuits were bypassed, and Self 2 was available instantly. Although this shift happened immediately, it was obviously going to take time for David's new volley to become a weapon he could count on. But at least he knew it was there.

PATIENT FILE

from Edd Hanzelik, M.D.

LOSS OF SELF

A patient, Brenda, was ill a great deal of the time. She went from one condition to another—allergies, fatigue, digestive distress, headaches. She was chronically in a state of sickness, and my best attempts didn't produce any improvement.

One day, Brenda came to the office accompanied by her mother, a very strong-willed, outspoken elderly woman. She managed to let everyone in the office know that Brenda had been obsessed with music as a child. All she wanted was to play music. But fortunately, she declared, she had convinced

Brenda that music was a silly occupation, and she should study to enter the world of business. "Now look at her," she announced loudly, pointing at her frail, sickly daughter. "She is an office manager, she makes a good income, she has a nice house. I've done a good job with her."

At this point, we could see that Brenda was spending her days making an office run smoothly when what she wanted was to make music. And suddenly a possible pathway to health opened up. Was there any doubt that Brenda's chronic condition was somehow related to her loss of self? It was sad to see this lovely young woman completely abdicating her own needs and desires—it was making her sick.

I asked Brenda if she still played music for her own enjoyment, and she replied that she didn't have much time for it, and listed her many obligations. Acting as a coach, I explored with her the possibility of making time to play music again. Brenda took to the idea quickly. We decided she would think of it as exercise, not for the muscles of her body, but for the muscles of her mind and spirit.

The next time Brenda came to the office, she seemed brighter, more energetic. She was already starting to feel better, and enthusiastically spoke of joining a musical group just for fun. I was happy to watch her move out of the stress system and into the realm of enjoyment and freedom, where health and well-being are much more likely. The simple task of pleasing oneself, of spending time in pure gratification and enjoyment, can open the door to healing. It's not magic, but it's a crucial beginning.

Self 1 piles on layers of judgment and fear, much like a piece of furniture that gets painted and varnished many times over. A furniture restorer comes along and begins to strip the layers. He is looking for the real finish. In the same way, over a lifetime, worries, judgments, and fears get layered on, so the question is, who is the real self? What do you find when you strip away all the concepts that are created by Self 1?

Over the years I have found that people have amazing inner abilities that are natural and productive. But they don't always have access to them when Self 1 is dominant. When I began to work with the doctors on using Inner Game techniques to address stress, it was like hitting the mother lode of Self 1. In our stress seminars, most people get it that they don't want to have those negative feelings and the resulting impaired performance. But for some it takes a lot to let go of the Self 1 habits of thought and be themselves.

INNER ABILITIES: THE QUALITIES OF YOUR SELF 2

One of the first questions we ask in the stress seminars is, "What are the natural inner abilities that you call on for support in difficult situations and can use in the course of everyday life?" We offer three guidelines for determining them:

1. They are qualities that are found in children.
2. We admire these qualities when we see them in others.
3. We like these qualities when we see them in ourselves.

Participants through the years have come up with surprisingly similar sets of core abilities and human powers. Here is a summary of what they say:

- To be aware and to feel
- To have courage and strength
- To have commitment and choice
- To enjoy and appreciate
- To love and be kind
- To hope and to trust
- To learn, understand, and find clarity

- To be creative and curious
- To be spontaneous and sincere
- To be happy and content

Many participants say they didn't realize they had so many inherent and positive capabilities, but, in fact, humans are hardwired to prefer stability, clarity, and peace to stress, fear, and frustration. And we all have the ability to develop these capabilities through reflection and self-discovery.

Of course, not all stress is related to performance. There is the stress of losing (or fearing the loss of) something precious to us. There is the stress of the conflict that arises in relationships. This is the stress of feeling unable to control one's environment or circumstances. These stressors are a part of everyone's life. The distinction is whether you relate to them from the perspective of Self 1 or Self 2. Self 2 is real, and Self 1 is largely illusion. But this illusion can run the show if we allow it to. Sometimes it is not obvious which self is which, so the Inner Game tools can help us make this important distinction. This is a distinction based on feelings, not on concepts or beliefs.

THREE

Meet Your Stress Maker

IN OUR STRESS SEMINARS, WE REFER TO SELF 1 AS THE STRESS MAKER. This nagging voice in our minds can create upheaval in any situation. As I described earlier, the Stress Maker is a familiar presence on the golf course. Golf can bring out the demons like few other games. It always amuses me that grown men and women, including myself, can place so much at stake in hitting a little white ball with a funny stick into a little round hole. But most do.

Recently, I was coaching Charlie, a charming, affable businessman, who seemed relaxed and happy to be on the golf course. He was a good golfer, usually scoring in the mid-eighties. As Charlie stood over the ball, he looked relaxed and poised. In fact, during his backswing and the beginning of his downswing, his composure was undisturbed. But as the club approached the ball, his demeanor transformed into a tight grimace that seemed almost violent and terrified at the same time. It was as if he were a different person during that split second. I wondered, "Who is this guy?

Where did Charlie go?" Then, a split second after impact with the ball, the composed face of easygoing Charlie was back.

I asked Charlie if he was aware of anything in particular going on with his lips during the swing. For the next few swings, he focused on this. He was a little embarrassed at what he observed, and gave a sheepish smile that told me he had recognized that his lips were tightening.

I pointed to his smiling face. "What do you think would happen if you let Charlie hit the ball? *This* Charlie. Not the scared guy who was making impact with the ball. I wonder what would happen."

Charlie got my point, but he seemed alarmed by the idea. "I don't know," he said. "I almost wouldn't dare. If *this* Charlie hit the ball, I'm afraid it would be a very wimpy shot."

I saw no need to inquire about why this change took place. I just wanted Charlie to be more aware and see what happened.

"Let's just see how wimpy it gets if you let Charlie hit the ball," I suggested. During the next shots the grimace gradually vanished as he saw in surprise that his balls were going considerably longer and straighter than before.

Charlie's story is a good example of what can occur in a moment of stress. Self 1, the Stress Maker, pictured the instant of striking the ball as a threat to its success. This image was enough to produce a physical reaction, and an interruption in the fluid motion of Self 2's swing. The simple task of the Inner Game is to bypass the Stress Maker so that Self 2 can shine.

THE STRESS MAKER'S VOICE

What is the Stress Maker in your life? What does it sound like? What we're calling the Stress Maker can also be called fear, doubt, confusion, and ignorance. We have all noticed times when we are able to handle the stressors of life without crumbling, while at other times the stress gets the best of us. The difference isn't only the degree of seriousness of the stressor, or our current state of stability. It's also how much we are influenced by the voices of the Stress Maker. Do you recognize the voice of *your* Stress Maker in the following?

• THE STRESS MAKER IS AN IDENTITY THIEF

It speaks as if it is speaking with your voice. For example, "I am such an idiot. . . . I can't do this. . . . I'm a failure. . . . No one likes me. . . . I'm worthless . . ." The Stress Maker makes judgments with such authority and knows you so well, you mistakenly accept its words as accurate self-assessment, even when they are not true.

PATIENT FILE

---

from Edd Hanzelik, M.D.

IDENTITY THEFT

When Ruth, a young woman in her thirties, first came to my office, she was desperately unhappy to the point of being suicidal. On the face of it, Ruth had every reason to be happy, but she couldn't find what she was looking for in life. She was consumed by a relentless inner dialogue led by the Stress Maker.

"I hate myself," she announced miserably during our first consultation.

"Wait a minute," I said, stopping her. "Who is the I?"

"I am the I," she said, looking puzzled.

"Are you sure that's you?" I asked. "That sounds like the Stress Maker talking. This could be a case of identity theft. Perhaps something has stolen your identity and is speaking as if it were you, and you are buying it."

Ruth was so surprised and intrigued that she briefly forgot her unhappiness for a while.

The moment of reflection created an opportunity to talk

with Ruth about her strengths as a person, and as a separate being from her voice of self-hatred.

Ruth's form of stress is the tyranny of negative concepts, which can dominate one's inner life. To overcome the tyranny, one must examine the source of the concept, question its merits, and discover the option to feel what psychologists have called unconditional self-regard.

I continue to see Ruth. We have looked at childhood experiences that contribute to her feelings of emptiness and self-loathing. She is relieved to recognize the voice of the Stress Maker as not *her*, and to see that she has a choice about whether or not to give the Stress Maker her deep respect and undivided attention. She recently expressed, with surprise and a big smile, that "It's been three months and I am still feeling good about myself."

• THE STRESS MAKER IGNITES CATASTROPHIC FEARS

The Stress Maker is skilled at anticipating the worst possible outcomes. For example, during your morning shower, you might notice a tiny lump on your neck. You think at first it's nothing serious, but the Stress Maker has other plans. It can immediately start imagining the worst possible diagnoses and the most frightening treatments. You start to push away the thoughts, but the Stress Maker takes advantage of the uncertainty of the situation to convince you of its fears. By the time you step out of the shower, you may be mentally experiencing the side effects of chemotherapy.

Fear has an energy all its own. It can paralyze common sense and critical thinking, while sending you into a flurry of counterproductive speculation. Here's an analogy. You're on a hike, and suddenly you feel a pain in your foot. Your mind starts agitating with possible causes. Maybe you have arthritis, maybe it's gout. Your imagination runs away with you as the pain grows worse. You ask a fellow hiker if he has some Advil or Tylenol, and you pop a couple of pills, but that doesn't offer much relief. You keep limping along. Maybe it's cancer, or something equally serious. Maybe your hiking days are over. As you entertain these thoughts, you become increasingly anxious and fearful. Your hike is virtually ruined.

Finally, one of the hikers says, "Hey, why not take off your shoe and see how your foot looks." So, you take off your shoe and find a small stone lodged under your toes. You take the stone out, and the pain subsides, along with the catastrophic fears. The Stress Maker draws from the pains of the past and creates the fears of the future.

PATIENT FILE

from John Horton, M.D.

UNDERSTANDING PAIN

Rebecca was referred to me for chronic back pain, which was debilitating. She had been unable to work for months, and yet there was no clear diagnosis, except a minor disc problem that did not explain the extent of her pain. She had been through courses of physical therapy and acupuncture, and nothing had improved her condition. As I sat with Rebecca and took her history, I could see how frightened she was by her pain.

Probing deeper, I learned that Rebecca's father had suffered from ALS, also known as Lou Gehrig's Disease. ALS is an excruciating and ultimately fatal disease, with a strong genetic component. As we talked about her father, I began to understand that Rebecca was terrified of inheriting ALS.

Fear of the unknown, and one's inability to control the future, can be a great source of anxiety. I explained to Rebecca that her pain had three parts. One was physical. The second was her fear of ALS. And the third was her generalized anxiety. Once she realized that fear and anxiety were producing greater pain than her minor back problem, she felt much better. And her problem completely resolved when she found out through genetic testing that she did not have the gene for ALS.

Subsequently, each time Rebecca had any sort of odd feeling in her back or legs, it no longer triggered her alarm system. These minor back pains, which never really responded to conventional therapies, were clearly not being caused by a spinal abnormality.

Excessive fear in itself is a cause of stress, whether the fear is realistic or not. The issue for anyone in pain is to get as clear a picture as possible of the causes of the pain, physically, mentally, and emotionally. This can take some time, but it's a major component in defeating crippling fear.

Exercise: Your Most Bothersome Fear

Without too much thought, jot down one of your most bothersome fears. See if you can identify anything about it that sounds like the exaggerations of the Stress Maker.

• THE STRESS MAKER PROMOTES NEGATIVITY

The Stress Maker has a capacity for Hollywood-like melodrama. With a single thought, such as "That person doesn't like me," it can unleash a cascade of negative emotions, including confusion, sadness, despair, anger, and fear. Once we've allowed the Stress Maker to convince us of something negative, it can seem very real.

There is an Indian story about a farmer whose mule breaks down. He decides to ask a neighbor if he can borrow his mule to plow his fields. But as he is walking to his neighbor's house, he starts imagining the critical things his neighbor is going to say—"Why can't you take care of your own mule? You could have prevented this. I don't want you to use my animal. I don't trust you to take care of it." He gets so worked up anticipating a negative response that as soon as his neighbor opens the door, he punches him and cries, "You bastard!"

That's the Stress Maker in action.

PATIENT FILE

from Edd Hanzelik, M.D.

UNDERSTANDING OLD TRAUMA

Meredith, a patient in her early sixties, was experiencing a burning sensation that cut through her entire body. The sensation was especially intense at night, keeping her awake. At first, her doctors thought her symptoms were related to menopause, and she was placed on a high dose of hormones, which only made things worse. She also had other symptoms, including digestive problems, fatigue, a lack of libido, depression, and panic attacks. By the time she came to me, she was desperate for answers.

I gave Meredith an in-depth evaluation, and we talked about her life. Her history was interesting. When she was twelve years old, she was riding in the backseat of a car going over the Brooklyn Bridge when she heard her mother shout, "Watch it!" The next thing she knew they were in the midst of a very severe car accident, with blood everywhere. Meredith's mother was dead.

Meredith had never fully explored her feelings about this traumatic event, and even talking to me almost fifty years later, she became tearful. I could see that Meredith probably had post-traumatic stress disorder from the experience. Her stress system had become hyperactivated at the time of the accident and it had never fully let go.

After eliminating the possibility of other illnesses, I explained to Meredith that her stress system was probably overstimulated and had been for some time. Not understanding that her symptoms were rooted in this childhood trauma, she had been at the mercy of the Stress Maker's exaggerated fears and negative suggestions.

At first it was difficult to provide treatment, because the first voice to respond from within Meredith was the voice of the Stress Maker, with its doubts, worries, and fears. As we began to focus on the healing of the emotional and physical trauma from the past, Meredith was able to get some distance from the Stress Maker and her physical symptoms began to improve.

We find in our medical practice that many chronic, debilitating symptoms begin to resolve when people see that they were created by old traumas. The Stress Maker's misinterpretation of the symptoms is capable of producing a great deal of anxiety. It's exciting to see symptoms improve when understanding replaces fear.

• THE STRESS MAKER IS A MASTER OF SELF-ATTACK

Self-attack is the trump card of the Stress Maker. It questions your every movement, insists on how bad you are, laughs at your desires, judges you mercilessly, and does it all in ways that convince you it is telling the truth.

The Stress Maker can keep you constantly on your toes with a steady chorus of coulds and shoulds, do's and don'ts: "You should have done this. You could have done that." Sometimes it will keep insisting you do something. When you finally do it, it will turn around and say, "Why did you do that?" It never seems satisfied with you. To say the least, it undermines your self-confidence.

The Stress Maker can be merciless. A wise friend of mine once said, "When human beings start judging themselves, the Devil would be kinder."

One derivative of self-attack is blame. Here is a poem, "The Sad Game," that Doctor Horton reads to some of his patients who are trapped in blame. It is by Hafiz, a fourteenth-century Persian poet, translated by Daniel Ladinsky:

> *Blame*
> *Keeps the sad game going.*
> *It keeps stealing all your wealth—*
> *Giving it to an imbecile with*
> *No financial skills.*
> *Dear one,*
> *Wise*
> *Up.*

PATIENT FILE

from Edd Hanzelik, M.D.

BYPASSING THE NEGATIVE VOICES

My patient, Rachel, was overweight and quite stressed. She was down on herself because of her weight. We began talking about her relationship with herself. I asked her to consider what she liked about herself, and to focus on that. Whenever she realized her mind was giving her a hard time about herself, I encouraged her to bypass that voice, not indulge it.

This was a new idea for Rachel. She asked, "You mean even if I can't turn off my negative thinking, I can bypass it?"

"Yes," I answered. "You cannot easily turn it off, because it is constantly running. But recognize it for what it is. You have a choice about whether you buy into it." I explained the nature of the Stress Maker and how we tend to give it tremendous respect. It knows how to present itself in a way that is extremely convincing. But we can step back and ask, "Do I agree with this? Is this in my best interest?" In general, self-attacks are never helpful. We can examine our own behavior with kindness and learn from it. We are all evolving and growing. But judgment and self-attack are counterproductive.

• THE STRESS MAKER CREATES FALSE EXPECTATIONS

The Stress Maker takes a typical concept—such as "Happiness is getting married, having two children, buying a house, and having a good job"—and insists that life be lived according to it. The Stress Maker can cause anguish and despair if one fails to measure up to these standards. The Stress Maker will tell you that you can't be beautiful unless you lose weight, that you can't be successful unless you achieve a certain level in your company, that you can't be worthy of admiration unless you live in a big house and drive a flashy car.

A study done recently in Orange County, California, a very wealthy area, revealed a high level of depression among the residents. When researchers investigated the cause for this, they found people with considerable wealth who were comparing themselves to others, not allowing themselves to feel satisfied because there were always others who had more than they did. One neighbor had bought a nicer car, and another neighbor had gone on a long cruise, and another had remodeled his house in a dramatic way. The researchers concluded that the stress caused by this chronic frustration was enough to explain the higher incidence of depression in this community.

The Stress Maker is full of concepts about what you should be. It reminds you of what you don't have and highlights the unfair ways you've been treated. For some, the Stress Maker is constantly suggesting that your dignity has been assaulted.

PATIENT FILE

from John Horton, M.D.

INSULT TO INJURY

Mark was retired, in his mid-sixties, and his life was good. He spent his time relaxing, playing tennis, and enjoying the fruits of his labor. He was very fit and somewhat narcissistic—very involved with himself and proud of his virility and health.

The Japanese have a saying that if a person never gets sick watch out, because when they eventually do they may not handle it well. This describes Mark.

Mark developed a little prostate problem, not uncommon for men his age. It wasn't a big deal, but he needed minor surgery to fix it. Mark was very upset about the prospect of an operation. He considered it an insult to his dignity. It challenged his self-image of being fit and healthy. He was deeply offended that such a thing should happen to *him*, a perfect specimen. But he agreed to the surgery because he didn't have much choice.

Mark's surgery was successful. His son and daughter-in-law were by his side, and I was there, too. I was surprised to see that although the surgery went well, Mark's state of mind was very poor. He was grumpy and irritable, verging on hateful. He was insulting to his family and to the nurses. Everyone was shaking their heads, wondering, "What's wrong with this guy? His surgery was quite successful."

Mark developed an infection in the hospital, which made him even more upset. How could *he* get an infection? He could not accept this. Now he was in a rage, and in spite of all our efforts, he didn't calm down and went into kidney failure.

It was very clear to both Mark's family and the medical staff that his healing was being seriously compromised by his attitude of hurt ego and the resulting stress. Tragically, Mark's condition continued to worsen, and he died. I learned a valuable lesson that if the Stress Maker is allowed to run the show, the best medical care can be sabotaged. Now, before a patient goes into surgery, I spend time working on how they are going to deal with it—what their self-image is in the midst of medical realities.

TAKING BACK CONTROL FROM THE STRESS MAKER

I've been self-employed for a long time. That hasn't stopped me from feeling nervous and upset sometimes about my work. One particular morning, I woke up and my first conscious feeling was anxiety. I had an intuition that I was letting the taskmaster part of my Stress Maker take charge. So I had a little dialogue with myself to see what was behind the anxiety.

> *"What's going on? Why are you so anxious?"*
>
> *"I know what's going to happen today! You're going to heap on all of these things for me to do—much more than I can possibly accomplish. And you're going to want them done at much higher standards and in less time than I'm really capable of. And then you're going to get down on me when I don't finish everything, and when I don't do it all perfectly."*

I realized then that I had been letting the Stress Maker run my workday. Realizing that this was the source of my stress made it easy to know realistically what could be accomplished during the day. The first step was to assure myself that I was in charge, not the demanding taskmaster.

Basically, it was a negotiation. I was telling myself, "Look, I have needs—things I have to accomplish today to put food on the table, but I'm going to protect us against the unrealistic expectations of the taskmaster part of the Stress Maker. Work with me here." I was choosing to build a protective shield, knowing that once the Stress Maker got me engaged, it could easily become my internal boss and put me in stress mode for the entire day. This choice was completely within my power.

In our stress seminars, we ask the participants for their ways of getting free of the Stress Maker. The class fills with excitement as people share their pet secrets for keeping the Stress Maker at bay. "I speak out loud, 'Stop! I'm not going there!' " one says. Another speaks silently to the Stress Maker: "Excuse me! You are not welcome here! I do not have time for you." A third person thinks of the possibility of colliding with a truck that day. The prospect of her life ending puts the Stress Maker's comments into proper perspective for her. And another simply ignores it and puts his attention on something else.

A friend of mine approached me and asked, "Do you know what worry is?"

"No. Tell me," I said.

"Worry is an imposter pretending to be useful."

I thought that was a useful definition.

The Stress Maker often shows up strongest in the face of the unknown, or in ambiguous situations where something could be this way or could be that way. The Stress Maker wants you to automatically buy into the worst. Self 2's alternative strategy is to explore. Find out the truth about the matter based on fact, and in actual proportion to your commitments in life.

Like the Wizard in *The Wizard of Oz*, the Stress Maker seems much more powerful than it truly is. It may look big and scary when you're first facing it, but once you step behind its screen, you discover how insignificant it actually is.

The key is to recognize the Stress Maker's voice for what it is. The first step is to say, "That's not me speaking. But I am the one listening." Then you can choose one of the many ways to bypass it rather than buy into it. Each time you do this, you take a big step toward winning the Inner Game of stress through your own wisdom.

The more you learn to differentiate the voice of the Stress Maker from yourself, the more natural and poised you feel, even in the face of stressors, and the greater access you have to your own wisdom. Using Inner Game tools may not make the Stress Maker's voice vanish, but your resistance to it develops like a muscle and your wisdom has a chance to grow.

Exercise: Bypass Your Stress Maker

Review the bothersome fear you noted above, and see if you can bring the Stress Maker down to size. How much of the fear is real, and how much is invented? What would *your* voice say to bypass the Stress Maker's concepts, rather than buy into them?

FOUR

An Alternative to Fight-Flight-Freeze

I'M VERY CLEAR THAT STRESS IS A FEELING I DON'T LIKE. WHEN I'M stressed out, I know I can't count on myself to think clearly or perform at my best. So I ask, a bit grumpily, "Why does stress even exist?"

My doctor friends have educated me about the stress system, which is a protective physiological adaptation from an earlier stage of human evolution that helped us survive. Our genes and our natural response mechanisms were shaped in a time when humans were basically hunter-gatherers. Think of those ancestors, gathering berries or relaxing after a meal. We see them in the present tense, like a film. Suddenly a huge predator leaps in their path. Their bodies respond instantaneously with a burst of adrenaline, like a car going from zero to sixty in five seconds. Their hearts start pumping, sending blood primarily to their muscles. This is the fight-or-flight response, which shifts all of the energy toward survival. There is no question that such a finely tuned physiological response has been essential to us in times of immediate danger.

I'm glad my ancestors had this stress system. Otherwise, I might not be here today. But it's clear to me that the system has gotten out of control, and is no longer helpful in most stress-producing situations that come up in the twenty-first century.

Today, most of us don't live in constant physical danger. We do, however, use the same stress system to cope with the dozens of minor stressors that fill our days—a harsh word from the boss, a toothache, a spat with a spouse, a missed train. These are open invitations for Self 1, the Stress Maker, to begin its chant and put its spin on the situation. If you are afraid of failure, even the smallest of tasks can be perceived as a stressor. Each perceived stressor sparks the release of hormones from the hypothalamus and the pituitary and adrenal glands. When too many of these hormones are circulating on a constant basis, it can have devastating effects.

Trying to live as a modern human while being defined by a primitive fight-or-flight instinct just doesn't work—as you can easily see if you've ever encountered road rage or been in an argument with a friend who responded by storming out of the room. While the stress response can still get us out of trouble if we're in true physical danger, our human capabilities have evolved beyond the fight-or-flight system. We possess innate resources that allow for more advanced responses. However, these resources are dormant in many people because we haven't learned how to access and develop them.

The effects of chronic stress can be insidious. For example, a study in Great Britain showed that people who feel wronged can really take it to heart—literally. In the study, people who thought life was unjust had 55 percent more coronary events, a greater rate than those with high cholesterol. Yet while doctors routinely test their patients' cholesterol levels, how many of them think to ask about their state of mind?

Here's the bottom line: Living in chronic stress is not possible without serious consequences. Edd and John have convinced me that the human body is not designed to handle or adapt to chronic stress.

Recently, I saw a PBS special on the work of Robert M. Sapolsky, professor of biology and neurology at Stanford University. Sapolsky wrote a book called *Why Zebras Don't Get Ulcers*, which looked at the profound impact of stress on humans' physical and psychological functioning. His TV special, based on his studies of baboon tribes in Africa, focused on one particular tribe that started feeding on the garbage from a safari camp and became exposed to tuberculosis. To Sapolsky's surprise, it was the strong alpha males who became sick and died. The less dominant males, females, and children survived. The tribe became more peaceful and thrived. Sapolsky speculated that the fierce competitive drive of the alpha males stressed them so much that they could not handle the tuberculosis germs as well as the others did. He also was struck with how well the baboons did in the absence of the communal stress of the fierce alpha males. Perhaps we could take a lesson from that in our own societies!

Exercise: What's at Stake?

Identify any situation that provokes prolonged stress. Reflect on how Self 1, the Stress Maker, might be seeing it as a matter of survival. What elements does Self 1 perceive as threatening? What does Self 1 think is at stake? What is really at stake?

PATIENT FILE

from Edd Hanzelik, M.D.

THE POWER OF FIGHT

Myra, a patient in her mid-sixties, came to the office because she was experiencing a quivering in her voice that was interfering with her ability to work. She knew the exact moment of onset: Myra had been home taking a shower. She had just stepped out and was drying herself, when she heard someone knocking on the door. She wrapped a towel around her body and started to go out, as the knocking became a pounding. Myra felt a surge of adrenaline.

The next thing she knew, two young men burst into her house. Myra was terrified; she described feeling as if her heart was extending out about two feet from her chest, pounding. She thought she was going to be raped and killed. Without planning it, Myra let out a yell from such a deep place that she was shocked to hear it. She said it sounded like the roar of a lion. She was amazed at the strength of the yell, and she was even more amazed that it was powerful enough that the two men turned and ran out of her house.

Following the incident, Myra was unable to speak at all for a couple of hours. When she began to speak, her voice was quivering. The state had persisted for several months. She had consulted an ear, nose, and throat specialist, who looked at her throat and reported that he could see her vocal cords trembling. She also saw a neurologist, who tried two different medications, both of which made the situation worse.

I viewed Myra's problem this way: Her profoundly threatened stress system had responded as it should, by immediately and powerfully saving Myra's life. Her vocal cords were not prepared for the lifesaving scream of the stress system and were traumatized. Emotionally, the entire experience had been traumatic. Often, while acute stress is happening, you don't notice the full impact on your body, because your focus is on survival. Then, when the stress is over and you start to relax, you discover how deeply your body has been compromised. When Myra let out the powerful scream, she didn't think about it or plan it. It was a spontaneous emergency response from her stress system. She was not even aware she was straining her vocal cords. However, when the threat was gone and she wanted to unwind, she became conscious of the quivering in her voice. Once a person has been traumatized by stress, the effect on the body, mind, and nervous system can persist, as it had for Myra.

For Myra, recovery started with the acknowledgment of the power of Self 2 to produce the scream in the first place, and the subsequent strain on her vocal cords. I asked her to give her voice rest, and to accept the emotional residue that was part of a normal response. I also asked her to recognize the inner resources that she had accessed in this emergency, and when she noticed the quivering, to thank her Self 2 (her innate body resources) for saving her. After a week, she came back saying she had rested her voice, noticed quivering several times, and had remembered her gratitude. Her voice gradually returned to normal.

DELIBERATE CALM

As we were writing this book, an event happened that made headlines around the world. On January 16, 2009, a plane taking off in New York City was struck by a flock of geese, disabling both engines and causing the plane to lose altitude rapidly. The pilot, the now famous Chelsey B. "Sully" Sullenberger, III, had to make an immediate decision, and he landed flawlessly on the icy Hudson River. All of the passengers were rescued by small boats already on the river. It was indeed the "Miracle on the Hudson."

What's interesting in the context of stress is that Sully was able to make a complex decision in the face of intense danger and fear. Pilots call this skill deliberate calm. Because accessing this skill requires conscious effort and regular practice, it is rehearsed over and over again in flight simulators.

What does conscious effort require? To understand, let's look at the biology of reactions that must have been occurring in Sully's body during the emergency. Although some might think he was not in a state of fear, this is not true—as he later confirmed. The fear circuitry of the brain is automatic, and it would have been activated in every person on the plane, including the well-trained pilot. This response comes from the more primitive brain centers, whose activation moves us into the typical stress reactions of fight or flight. As the plane plunged toward the river, the experience of overwhelming fear was unavoidable.

So, we know that Sully was afraid. But we also know that he was able to balance his automatic emotions with a more rational and deliberate thought process, which is centered in the prefrontal cortex of the brain. It was this ability that enabled him to quickly examine many possible variables, make a wise decision about the best place to land, and perform skillfully. Sully was able to access a more advanced system of brain structure and function. He could move from a fear-based response to draw on what he had learned from his experience as a pilot.

Much of our experience of stress is based on primitive reactions. But, like Sully, we can learn to be more effective pilots of our lives by drawing on the advanced neurocircuitry that we have evolved as human beings.

PATIENT FILE

from John Horton, M.D.

FLIGHT FROM PAIN

The fattest man I ever met was a patient I saw as a consultant at a clinic in San Francisco. Larry, who weighed over four hundred pounds, was determined to lose weight. His story is unique and extreme, but it has implications for the epidemic of obesity in the United States and other countries.

Larry had never been particularly overweight growing up,

and no family members had weight problems. His weight gain occurred as his response to a singular event—the death of his wife and child in the famous Jonestown mass suicide. Larry, a successful businessman, had been at home in Los Angeles raising funds for the Jonestown group. He and his wife believed that the group held promise for a new idealistic way of life. When the mass suicide occurred, Larry lost not only his wife and child, but also his vision of a life of purpose and service.

In a small voice he told me that his immediate response to this event was to call out for some pizza. As he was eating the pizza, Larry dialed up a local fried chicken place. As he was eating the chicken, he made another call to a Chinese takeout restaurant, and while he was eating that food, he considered what kind of pizza he would order next.

For weeks Larry numbed his pain with food. He then started wandering the streets at night, following women with children who reminded him of his wife and children. He meant no harm. One day he chanced to see himself in a mirror and was shocked to see a massive, distorted monster who did not resemble anyone he knew.

He realized that he had been sedating himself with food to avoid the pain of his loss. In a way, overeating worked to reduce his stress in the moment, but did nothing to relieve the source of his stress. In fact, it caused him to have a serious medical condition. Slowly he began to feel and not eat, and had lost about one hundred pounds by the time I met him. He had another one hundred pounds to go.

As Larry told me his story, I was impressed with his courage, and his willingness to experience his losses and regain himself. At the end of the consultation we both had confidence that Larry would gradually rediscover himself, sadly without his wife and child, but wiser and more conscious.

This was a profound lesson for me in how powerful the primitive stress system can be, and how necessary it is to resolve the cause of stress rather than cover it up by any means available, including overeating, drugs, or excessive alcohol. Seeing Larry's resolve was encouraging to me and gave me hope that people caught in even the most extreme cycles of numbness can find their way back to themselves.

FREEZE: A DEER IN THE HEADLIGHTS

Edd and John suggested that there is another primitive response in addition to fight or flight. This is the freeze reaction—literally what happens to a deer caught in the headlights. The deer is not really running or fighting. It is just frozen in the moment, paralyzed with fear. I understood the concept of freeze immediately. I had often seen it on the tennis court. When players at the net saw a speeding ball coming toward them, and weren't sure what to do, they'd often just stand there, paralyzed, as the ball whizzed by them.

The freeze reaction is another automatic response from the nervous system, which is conditioned to meet some dangers with a lowering of blood pressure and heartbeat. This reaction may seem counterintuitive, but if you think back in the evolutionary order of things, sometimes being as still as possible was the best option. The intent was to be invisible.

The freeze reaction reminds me of being a small child lying in bed with the lights off. You know that the monsters have come from their hiding place in the closet, out into the room. You can't yell or run because then they'll see you and get you. You certainly can't fight them because they are monsters. So what you do is you become very, very little. You slow down your breathing so that in a sense you don't exist. You become invisible.

Adult forms of freezing include getting stuck in unproductive patterns, not wanting to deal with difficult situations, and taking no action when action is called for.

In their practice, John and Edd have found that people who suffered traumatic or abusive childhoods tend to have the habit of freezing at times when it's not so beneficial. They described a young architect who had unexpectedly fainted when an upset colleague was telling him about a serious illness. He was taken to the emergency room, but no cardiac or neurological illness was discovered to explain his symptoms. He also had no idea why he had collapsed. However, when John Horton asked him if any physical, mental, or emotional stress had happened in his childhood, he recalled coming home one day to find his mother being attacked by his uncle. His mother died from the attack. Thereafter, for this young man, any strong emotion triggered a severe stress reaction, which, in his case, was to freeze. Talking about the experience was difficult for him. However, he realized that earlier on the day he collapsed at work, a colleague had been sharing a very emotional story with him, and her intense emotion had triggered his response.

This man's learning process was interesting. Although he had gained a clear understanding of why he had fainted, some time after he again fainted while on an airplane. But this time he realized that he was under emotional stress, was tired, and hadn't eaten well. He understood that stress was triggering his old freeze reaction, and he chose to bypass it. He recovered quickly and didn't need to go to the hospital. He recognized that his nervous system had a certain vulnerability that he could deal with without fear, confusion, or unnecessary medical workups.

Exercise: Being Frozen

Think of a situation in which you have experienced the freeze reaction or have seen others experience it. What was the result of freezing?

MEDICAL NOTE: OUR THREE BRAINS

John Horton, M.D., and Edward Hanzelik, M.D.

The Inner Game allows us to switch as needed from instinct to wisdom. The following simple description can help you understand the brain's structure and functions involved. When we present this information in seminars, participants appreciate seeing how the brain reacts when we choose to respond in more evolved ways beyond the fight-flight-freeze reactions. Let's look at it from an evolutionary perspective, based upon the novel theory of scientist Paul MacLean and more recent research.

MacLean saw that we have three brains, with the younger ones layered on top of the older ones. He speculated that illness could occur when the primitive brain centers dominate our more advanced human brain centers. When this happens, instead of having access to reason and understanding, we react to human affairs in animalistic and primitive ways. Some characterize civilization as only a veneer of human behavior over a core of these primitive behaviors. However, if we consider the uniquely human qualities and the remarkable capacities of the human brain to express them, we see clearly that we have the potential to be a lot more than just sophisticated animals.

MacLean called the first, most primitive, brain the reptilian brain. It is focused on individual survival and knows neither friend nor family nor fun. In humans this consists of the brain stem, which maintains the vital functions of life, including heartbeat, breathing, and metabolic activity, and the cerebellum. Even when extensive brain injury occurs, if these areas are preserved, life can continue. The behaviors of this part of the brain are very resistant to change, tend be grounded in fear, and are not capable of learning. This part of the brain is

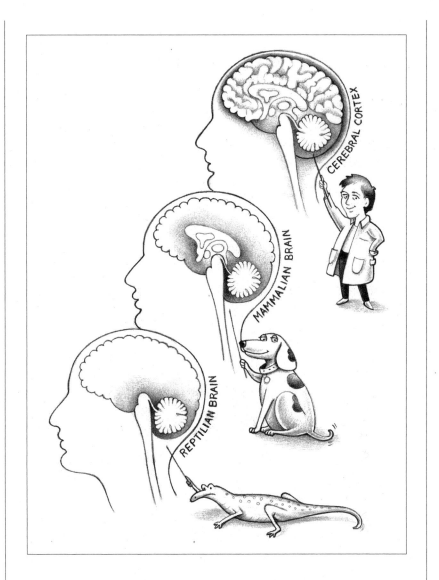

quite limited in its response to challenges. Reptiles (or humans operating in the reptilian mode), when perceiving threat, only attack, flee, or freeze.

MacLean called the second brain the mammalian brain. It includes the amygdala, a more refined sentry for danger than exists in the reptilian brain. The amygdala joins with the hypothalamus, the pituitary, and the adrenal glands to coordinate our most basic fight-flight-freeze responses to protect us from harm. The amygdala is activated automatically, without thought. For example, imagine you walk out your front door, and you see a shape on the grass that looks like a snake. You immediately jump back with fear. Then you look more closely and see that the shape is actually a garden hose. You relax, laugh, and go on your way. The initial reaction was the instinct of the early mammalian brain, including the amygdala. If that's all you had, you might have attacked or run away from the garden hose.

Our more evolved mammalian brain has a more sophisticated sentry, the hippocampus, capable of refined perceptions and feelings. It was the hippocampus that helped you realize the garden hose was not a snake. The hippocampus has the capacity for learning and memory, which gives mammals additional abilities. Unlike a reptile, your pet dog recognizes and responds to you, and obviously makes the distinction between you and a stranger.

The third, highest, component is the human brain, which includes the large cerebral cortex, making up five-sixths of the brain. This is our thinking brain, with numerous connections between the hippocampus and the prefrontal cortex. The prefrontal cortex connects many large neural networks that allow for the various qualities of human thought, reflection, and wisdom.

The cerebral cortex is involved with most advanced mental activities including speech, rational thought, memory, understanding, fine motor control, creativity, musical ability, writing, empathy, kindness, the ability to be part of a family or group and still be an individual, awareness of the story of your own life, and the recognition of time.

Most of the stress we experience cannot be handled well by the primitive brain, with its fight-flight-freeze reactions, or by the ancient or more advanced mammalian brains, with their limited capacities governed by instinct, group conformance, and pecking order. Only by accessing our unique human brain can we step back, reflect, and take conscious action.

The human brain has the capability to balance the more primitive reactions of the stress system with wisdom and understanding. Access to our human brain allows us to laugh in the face of threat, and to design brilliant strategies to resolve and transcend pain and frustration. We have the potential to outsmart life's challenges.

BEYOND THE STRESS PERCEPTION

The three of us live in Southern California, and we have experienced the frightening wildfires that, driven by high winds, can sweep through the canyons of Malibu and destroy homes in a few hours. There's no question that the wildfires are a tremendous stressor. However, even this great stressor does not in itself *cause* stress. To illustrate a key feature of the psychology of stress, imagine three people standing on a canyon road watching towers of angry flames approach the two houses in front of them.

One man is a firefighter, engaged in a strategy of defense against the fire. He is exhilarated, and completely engaged in directing helicopters arriving with water to stop the spread of the fire. The second man, a homeowner, is nervous but not afraid. He has owned his house for many years, and has seen other fires. He has good insurance, and he's prepared to take all people, pets, and important valuables in one trip in his van if the water from the helicopters does not stop the fires. The third man is also a homeowner, but he is overwhelmed with terror. His home is newly purchased, and he doesn't know if he has good insurance. He cannot possibly take all his people, pets, and valuables to safety in his small car. The three men face the same stressor, but their perception of the stressor and their responses to it are completely different.

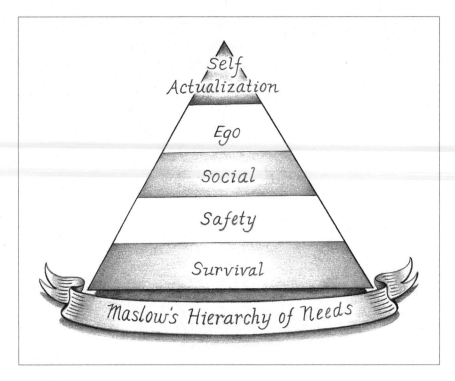

Psychological stress has to do with perceptions that frustrate a person and cause pain or fear. This is true whether the perceptions are grounded in reality or not. In the above example, the fire may not harm the two houses, but the third man might continue to feel stressed for some days, or even weeks and months. The other two are protected from fear of the fire by training, experience, and contingency planning.

Another psychological aspect of stress is more subtle. This has to do with the frustration of our human need for self-actualization. Psychologist Abraham Maslow, in his hierarchy of human needs, listed self-actualization as the highest need. He discovered that the most successful and mentally healthy people were fulfilling this need. We have an innate longing to progress in our lives to a point where we are satisfied with ourselves and with what we've achieved. We may not realize it, but we yearn for inner contentment. Without appreciating this most human of needs, we are less than ourselves, and this lack can be a source of stress.

The psychologist Carl Jung observed that his patients who were most afraid of death were those who felt that they had never fully lived. The opposite is also true. People who have lived fully and found inner contentment are more at peace in the face of their mortality.

SOS: THE SOCIOLOGY OF STRESS

Our world is composed of three dynamic relationships: the relationships with one's self, with others, and with society—SOS for short. Stressors can come from any of these arenas, but the relationship to self is the key to regulating our stress system. Why? Because it is the one arena where we can always exert control. We can't control what other people think, feel, or do; nor do we have much control over the input we get from society. But in our own protected selves, we have room to maneuver, as long as we're willing to face things as they are and take advantage of our unique inner resources.

Appreciating the need for self-understanding can be difficult, as we are social beings. The question is, how can you be a part of the herd and not lose yourself in the process? How can you remain connected to something larger than yourself—your family, your community, your work team—and still remain able to step back and keep your own counsel?

Confucius is quoted as saying that when he was young he tried to please his parents, later to please his friends, and still later to please his wise teachers. Finally, he learned to please himself. That's when he discovered the inner wisdom that has had such a profound effect on Chinese culture.

Compulsive people-pleasing is a common problem, and one that allows for little success. There is a very famous story of the Hindu deity Shiva and his consort, Parvathi, which illustrates this point. Parvathi asked Shiva why, although the earth was so beautiful and human beings were designed to enjoy it, they tended to be so unhappy. Shiva asked Parvathi to accompany him to earth.

They disguised themselves as humans and watched an ordinary elderly couple go along a path from one little village to another. First, he rode on a donkey and she walked beside him. As they reached a village, they heard the villagers say how selfish and mean the man was, to be riding while his poor wife walked. As they approached the next village, he got off and she rode the donkey while he walked. Again, the villagers were very critical, saying that this woman had no respect for the man who had worked so hard all his life, and that he should be riding. So, when they approached the next village, both sat on the donkey. The villagers were appalled that they could be so cruel to burden the poor donkey with all that weight. So at the next town, they got down and both walked alongside the donkey. At which point the villagers derided them for their foolishness. They had a healthy donkey and no one was riding it!

After observing this episode, Shiva looked at Parvathi and said, "You see, human beings so much want to please one another, and yet it is impossible." And while it's part of human kindness to want to please others, nothing is gained if we lose ourselves in the process.

A STEP IN HUMAN EVOLUTION

If stress has an evolutionary origin, then it stands to reason that there is another step in human evolution that can help us survive the current onslaught of stressors. When Edd, John, and I use the Inner Game tools in our seminars, we find that a fundamental shift occurs in the way participants function. Instead of the fear, surprise, and shock with which most people receive the inevitable but still surprising changes of life, we see them learning fresh responses, which take advantage of the inner abilities of Self 2— reactions such as clarity, love, learning, awareness, and acceptance. When we recognize the old stress system responses, we can discover the choice we have for more evolved options.

The challenge is that the primitive stress response is automatic and survival-based. It can be turned on in our bodies without our conscious awareness. It is like exercising muscles we haven't exercised before; it takes daily effort to develop strength and flexibility.

Exercise: Using Your Higher Brain

Consider one of the stressful situations you chose in Chapter One, and your usual response to it. Stop and reflect on alternative responses to fight-flight-freeze, given the qualities available from the human brain.

FIVE

Gearing Up and Gearing Down

THE STRESS WE ENCOUNTER IS NOT INHERENT. WHEN I WAS TEACH-ing tennis and golf, I was always struck by how people got very stressed doing an activity that was supposed to be recreation. They'd say, "I'm going to relax and play some tennis . . ." or, "I want to take a break and hit the golf course." But they'd get there and wham, they were more charged up than they'd been before. They were supposed to be gearing down, but they were actually gearing up. I often observed people on the golf course on a beautiful sunny day, with the green stretching out in front of them, surrounded by their friends. They had everything they needed for enjoyment, but their faces told a different story—of grim concentration, disappointment, resentment. No wonder cardiac arrest is the number one cause of death on the golf course. The stress we encounter is not inherent to the games of tennis or golf. It comes from the meaning we attribute to winning and losing, to playing well or not playing well. Making a conscious choice about this meaning is part of transcending harmful stress. Since the rules of golf say nothing about its meaning, it is up to the players to invent that meaning. To make this choice consciously is to ask yourself not only what your golf goal might be, but why you are playing the game on any given day. What is your purpose? What is your intention? You might choose to play for exercise, or for the camaraderie of your playing partners, or to just get away from it all and enjoy the beauty of the course. It is also possible to choose to learn something about yourself, to practice focus of attention, or to experiment with the power of making a choice about the meaning you are going to give to the game that day. You might find that it is not so easy. The unconscious influence of the meaning given by society and friends will want to take over. You'll need to keep rehearsing your stated intention: "No, I'm not here today to prove my prowess, I'm here to _____."

GEARING DOWN

We all spend our days gearing up and gearing down, and most of the time it's unconscious. The problem comes when chronic fear or frustration, or being overwhelmed, leads to exhaustion. It is not rocket science to observe this in ourselves. When we're overstressed, we're like the dry sponge that has too little liquid yet is still being squeezed. Unable to accommodate, we begin to tear. The point is to be aware enough to know when it's time to gear up and when it's time to gear down. It's a matter of making conscious decisions.

If instead of gearing down we overuse stimulants or other artificial means to keep going, we can get exhausted even more quickly. Gearing down is a human need, just as crucial as gearing up. Rest, relaxation, recreation, and reflection are all means of gearing down which are essential to our stability and well-being.

Think about what happens to an individual in a typical day. So many situations can feel stressful. Driving to work and getting stuck in a traffic jam—stressful. Arriving at work and feeling a lack of control, a lack of appreciation, too much to do, too little time—stressful. Coming home, being faced with complex interpersonal problems—stressful. Sitting down, watching the evening news, seeing all the terrible things happening in the world—stressful. Then we go to sleep—or try to. This is the time when our bodies, geared up all day long, have a chance to gear down and recover. But since it is easier to gear up than it is to gear down, this restful period may be tough to achieve. Sleep disturbances are all too common a problem in modern life.

A good example of the dynamic is jet lag. We know that it is a real phenomenon. When you cross time zones traveling from one distant place to another, your physical body is there, but your physiological processes take time to come into line. Your digestive system will take longer to adjust than your musculoskeletal system. You can generally get up and do what you need to do, but normal eating and digestion take longer. Fine coordination takes longer than general coordination. Mental faculties take longer still, and emotional responses lag behind everything else. So, here is a body that has hurdled through space and arrived somewhere ten or twelve hours later, but it's a temporarily compromised body.

In America, the cultural default is to push ourselves past our limits. We operate like a souped-up Volkswagen that has been given a 400-horsepower engine that keeps going and going and going. The engine is so powerful that over time it breaks down the rest of the car. Fenders are falling off, the hood has cracked, windows are breaking. Finally, the whole car is just a shambles, except that the engine is still going. The mind can be like that 400-horsepower engine, and the body like the more fragile Volkswagen it's pushing around. This is the way we treat ourselves by failing to gear down and find a workable cruising speed.

PATIENT FILE

from John Horton, M.D.

RUNNING ON EMPTY

A patient of mine owns a gym. One day he asked me if I would be willing to take care of some of the "gym rats" who were sick a lot of the time. I started seeing these patients and found that they couldn't recover from simple colds and flus because they insisted on doing a few hours of very-high-impact aerobic exercise every day. Their justification was that exercise made them feel good, and without it they felt lost. As one man put it, "I get depressed when I don't exercise. Exercise helps me deal with the stresses of life."

However, it was clear to me that this intense level of exercise was actually counterproductive for this group, as it didn't allow them the chance to heal from illness. The immune system needs some space and energy to develop antibodies that defeat viruses, and the sick gym rats were unwilling to allow the process to happen. They really wanted me to prescribe more and different antibiotics, which would not have been effective against chronic viral infections.

In the end, I was not able to help them, because they were completely sold on the false idea that they needed to be constantly geared up to cope with life. They didn't believe in the value of gearing down. They didn't understand their own inner resources. Their commitment to exercise overrode the signals from their bodies that were telling them, "Slow down . . . rest." In a sense, they were addicted to their own endorphins.

The endorphins our bodies produce when we're geared up can feel good, and if we're constantly geared up, we come to rely on them. From an evolutionary point of view, endorphins are valuable. When our ancient ancestors, living in dangerous jungles, were slashed or bitten by predators, the release of endorphins allowed them to bypass the pain. Sometimes we "feel no pain," even though our bodies are exhausted and getting ill.

Medical research and common sense show that appropriate exercise makes us more resilient to stress and improves health overall. The question arises, what is *appropriate* exercise? The gym rats were using extreme exercise as their only remedy for stress. But exercising for health is not the same as an athlete reaching for high performance. When the goal of exercise is health, one critical variable is enjoyment, but these people were torturing themselves. They were obsessed with working out at the cost of developing other abilities to cope.

LIVING ON OVERLOAD

The most common complaint I hear at corporations and in our stress seminars is that people feel overloaded. There are just too many obligations and demands. I find it ironic that new technologies, designed to make work more efficient, have had the opposite effect. Many people complain that they are overwhelmed by the need to respond to a barrage of e-mails each day. One manager told me that when she returned from a three-day vacation, there were four hundred e-mails waiting for her! What could be more stressful than the pressure to accomplish more than is humanly possible? But that's what many people face, and when I ask them what they can do to regain some control, they look at me as if I'm nuts and say, "If I want to keep my job, I have no choice."

So here's the predicament: It isn't remotely possible for you to do what you've been asked, but you are expected to do it anyway, and you have no choice in the matter. If you keep going this way, you're going to crash. It's inevitable.

MEDICAL NOTE: THE COMMITMENT TO BALANCE

Edward Hanzelik, M.D., and John Horton, M.D.

How committed is your body to staying in balance? Walter Cannon, an eminent physician and medical researcher, wrote a fascinating book on this subject in 1932, called *The Wisdom of the Body*. It remains a classic of clarity and understanding today. Dr. Cannon explored the extraordinary actions the body takes to stay in balance, or homeostasis, regardless of what challenges are presented to it.

As an example of how important balance is to life, consider our need for oxygen. If we are deprived of oxygen for more than a few minutes, we will have irreversible damage to the nerve cells of our brain, and death will soon follow. When we do vigorous physical exercise, our need for oxygen can rise forty-five-fold, yet our maximal ability to take in oxygen may only be able to rise twelve-fold. How will the body respond when it needs such a vital substance as oxygen, but cannot take in anywhere near enough to fulfill its needs?

Cannon discovered that numerous other actions were taken by the body to ensure that its need for oxygen was supported, even under the most demanding circumstances. The frequency of breaths increases dramatically, pulling a lot more oxygen into the lungs. The volume of blood pumped by the heart increases. The rate of the heartbeat accelerates. Blood pressure rises. Oxygen crosses into the capillaries with greater ease. Tissues become more capable of extracting oxygen from the blood. And there is even a sudden increase in the body's ability to manufacture red blood cells to carry the oxygen. All of these remarkable changes constitute the dramatic responses of the body to a major challenge. The net effect is that balance is maintained and our tissues get a consistent supply of oxygen.

Cannon looked at every system in the body from this perspective, including fluid balance, salt, blood sugar, proteins, blood calcium, body temperature, and others. He discovered that there are similar elaborate mechanisms built into all of the body's systems to protect homeostasis, regardless of the physical challenge.

But what if the challenge to homeostasis is created in the mind or emotions? What happens when chronic stress throws off the balance of multiple systems of the body? When imbalances are caused by chronic stress, we can't just sit back and await the body's efforts to get back to balance. We have to express conscious awareness and choice. We must implement the necessary steps to maintain our balance. The more we practice this, the more natural and habitual it becomes. The Inner Game's understandings and tools help us see clearly that we do have a choice and that we do have access to amazing inner resources that enable us to maintain our stability, whatever life brings our way.

A few years ago, I got myself into a situation where I had accepted too many obligations. When I took an objective look at my to-do list, I saw that I had committed 250 percent of my time. I felt like an overbooked airline—too many bodies, not enough seats. How had I allowed this to happen? It was easy. People had approached me with ideas that interested me, and I'd said yes because I really wanted to pursue them, but I forgot to check in with the reality of limited time.

Most of the people who come to our stress seminars say they have too much to do. More often than not, their response to this crunch is to sacrifice sleep, relaxation, and recreation, because they view these as being expendable. But as we saw earlier, gearing up without gearing down is the worst thing you can do for your health.

Can you release yourself from the tyranny of the undones on your to-do list? Do you have a choice?

I have never met a person who, given the choice, would not want (and, consequently, need) more time for rest and reflection. Therefore, I have to conclude that the dilemma is one of freedom. Do we have the freedom to have more of what we want and need? This is not freedom *from*, but freedom *for*.

PATIENT FILE

from John Horton, M.D.

AN EASY TARGET

Roy, a health-conscious middle-aged executive, came to see me during his Christmas vacation. He had a badly infected scratch on his face from shaving, and it was threatening to spread, even to his brain. We were able to treat it with several days of intravenous antibiotics in the hospital. Roy did very well, but he was disturbed by this unexpected illness from a simple nick on his face. "How could I get so sick from such a tiny bacterial infection?" he asked me. The answer was simple. For months Roy had been overworking and resenting it. He was unhappy at work, pushing himself hard to finish projects he didn't believe in. Without time to rest, it was predictable that his body would give out in some way. It wasn't necessarily the workload that pushed Roy to the limit. It was the stress of a work environment that was unfulfilling.

Hans Selye, who wrote the classic book *The Stresses of Life*, and whose theories are still used in medical research today, discovered that the body will adapt to prolonged stress by gradually increasing the activity of the sympathetic nervous system—the fight-flight-freeze response. Over a long period of adaptation, the metabolic systems will become exhausted, causing burnout. Selye saw that disease, and eventually death, can occur if balance is not restored.

To illustrate, consider what would happen if you lightly stroked your forearm with two fingers. It would not be an unpleasant experience. But what if you continued to do it day after day, for a week, or a month? The skin on your forearm would wear down; eventually, a sore would develop. In the same way, chronic stress develops gradually over time, eventually wearing away our reserves and creating illness.

Selye also observed that even in the state of near-exhaustion, people will engage in activities that stimulate them and keep the sympathetic nervous system revved up, rather than respond to the body's clear message that it needs rest. It's like whipping a tired horse to get him to run faster. People fight fatigue with coffee, tea, caffeinated soft drinks, cigarettes, alcohol, and high-fat food. Stimulants further weaken the body and create greater imbalance.

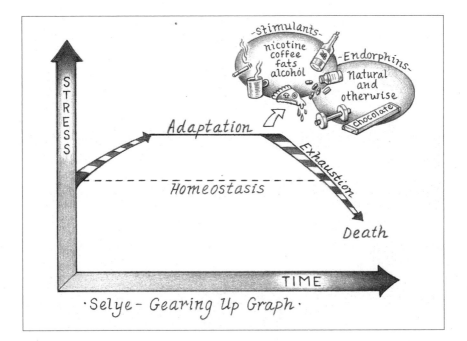

·Selye- Gearing Up Graph·

THE FOUR R'S

Many of us live our lives in attack mode. We attack the project, we attack the tennis ball, we attack the daily chores. We see threats and enemies. We are hypervigilant. We're in a jungle of our own creation, with the saber-toothed tigers threatening. By now I hope you're starting to get it that being in attack mode isn't going to get you very far for very long.

Edd and John have had a lot of success coaching their patients in the four R's—rest, relaxation, recreation, and reflection. At first, people have a hard time understanding that these factors are not just "nice to have," but are absolutely essential to life and health. Sometimes it takes a major physical breakdown before they see the light.

When we ask people in the stress seminars how much of their week they devote to rest, relaxation, recreation, and reflection, they get bent out of shape. They can't remember, can't identify the times. Life is just too busy and overpowering. Other responses are interesting. For example, Cynthia, a woman in one seminar, when asked what she did to relax and unwind, replied, "I watch TV." I asked, "What do you watch?" She went on to describe how she was addicted to the news and talk shows that were obsessively following the plight of a missing three-year-old girl who was presumed to have been murdered. Every evening, she devoted two or three hours to the details. Someone else in the group said, "I don't know who you're talking about. I haven't heard this story." Cynthia sighed and said, "I envy you." Even as she spoke the words, she realized that she had a choice to turn off the TV.

John likes to tell the story of the time he worked in Taiwan. Every day after lunch, the whole society shut down for a rest. It was a hard adjustment for John because he grew up in a society that said, "If you need a nap, you're a wimp." But he came to see the cultural wisdom in their quiet time. In our culture, if you suggested that everyone take a nap after lunch, they'd laugh you out of the room. We're doers to the extreme. The hardest workers eat lunch at their desks. They keep going and going. Managers want to know how they can squeeze more productivity out of people in every minute of the workday. In some companies, people vie to be the last one to leave the office at night.

PATIENT FILE
_____

from John Horton, M.D.

WHAT A BODY NEEDS

Susan came for an evaluation because she was experiencing heart palpitations at night. Susan was a young woman, and it seemed unlikely that she had heart disease—an observation that was confirmed after a thorough physical workup. I mentioned that sometimes palpitations can be caused by excessive caffeine or excessive stress. Susan said that caffeine wasn't a problem, but admitted that her very full life had been made more full recently. She had taken on a volunteer position in the community, and it had turned out to be much more demanding than she'd expected.

My instinct was that an effective prescription for Susan needed to include the four R's—rest, relaxation, recreation, and reflection. I told Susan, "I think we can resolve your problem rather easily."

She brightened and looked at me eagerly. I smiled. "I have to warn you, when I tell you what you need to do, you might laugh because it seems so absurd."

"Oh, no," she insisted. "I won't laugh. I trust your advice."

"Okay," I said, "if you could take a half hour each day simply for yourself, just to sit down and do whatever you please, very soon your problem will be addressed."

Susan laughed.

I left her in the examination room and said I'd meet her

back in my office. When I walked into my office a few minutes later, I was shocked to find Susan sitting in a chair sobbing. Concerned, I asked her if I had said something that hurt her feelings.

She shook her head and wiped her eyes. When she could speak, she said simply, "I didn't realize how bad it was." She explained that she'd been unable to conceive of having even a half hour in the day just to do anything she pleased. And she was beginning to realize that her situation was not compatible with a well-functioning body. It's remarkable how many patients we find suffering from stress and illness who believe there is no time to take care of themselves. Of course, they end up spending much more time dealing with the consequences of stress.

Exercise: Reflecting on the Four R's

Write down your preferred methods of engaging in rest, relaxation, recreation, and reflection. Include breaks, jogging, games, sports, just kicking back, nonbusiness conversations, and other activities. Note the approximate time you give yourself per week for each of the four R's.

How would you assess the sufficiency of time you have allotted? Do you notice an insufficiency in any area? What are the consequences? What corrective action could you take?

PURPOSEFUL EXERCISE

When people talk about reducing stress, they usually list the common methods they've been taught—exercise, deep breathing, and so on. But outer strategies are effective only when the Inner Game is being played well. For example, in our seminars, people often mention exercise as a good way to reduce stress. We know that's what their doctors tell them: "If you want to reduce stress, you have to exercise." Good advice, right? Well, that depends. We present people with three different examples of exercise. In the first, a person is on a treadmill at a gym watching television. In the second, a person is jogging on the beach in the morning. In the third, a person is walking across a field in the evening to visit a friend for a drink and a chat at the end of the day.

Which activity is healthier? Keep in mind that all three are burning the same number of calories and working the same muscles. People usually think that if the physical activity is the same, all three are benefiting similarly. That's the outer game. But if you look beyond that to the other areas that enhance health, you can see that the person jogging on the beach might reap an additional benefit from appreciating the beauty of nature, and the person walking to meet a friend not only enjoys the beauty of nature, but also has the additional benefit of making a human connection.

A busy corporate lawyer who was taking our seminar mentioned that he had such a hard time scheduling time for exercise that he hired a personal trainer to come to his home and bought some equipment for a home gym. One morning, while he was working with the trainer, he looked outside. It was a beautiful day, and his gardener was doing the yard work. He had a revelation. "I realized that I was paying my trainer to exercise me, and paying for equipment, and I was also paying my gardener. I thought that perhaps if I did some of the gardening myself, I would accomplish three purposes—not paying for the trainer or the equipment, enjoying outdoor exercise, and enjoying the improvement in my garden."

STABILITY VS. STRESS

Now you've seen the actual physical and emotional consequences of stress, and you may have recognized yourself in some of the stories. In this book, we are not suggesting that you try to fight stress, or even to manage it. Instead, the overall strategy is to build stability. Stability is that which resists being toppled by stress. It is a dynamic state of being that allows us to move in our desired direction. Stability is of great value whether or not we happen to be in stress. If chronic stress is the absence of stability, it stands to reason that building stability will automatically mitigate stress. Fortunately, the preference for stability over the imbalance of stress is built into us and makes our choice easier.

The first step is a commitment based on understanding that stress is not good for you and you want to build inner stability. This commitment is not easy in a world that thinks stress is something to be tolerated as a normal consequence of working and being in relationship with others. This step of commitment is a choice to evolve beyond being bullied by stress. It's a choice to value and protect your life and to live in balance, even if your external world is in crisis. You could say it's a choice of the heart to appreciate and enjoy your life no matter what.

Tools are offered in this book that help build inner stability and enable you to live with an internal integrity that holds you true to yourself in the face of the external changes and demands that normally compromise one's ability to perform, enjoy, and learn. Stability is more than surviving, having a good job, and enjoying a family. It is an inner strength sourced in understanding and wisdom. To make this commitment practical, we'll look at the foundations of stability in the next section.

PART TWO

OUTSMARTING STRESS

SIX

The Inner Game Learning Code: ACT

EVERY SPRING A DRAMA GOES ON OUTSIDE OF MY HOUSE. THE sparrows build their nests in the bushes and trees and lay their eggs. When the eggs hatch, the baby sparrows are no bigger than my thumb. Then the predators come—starlings, ravens, occasionally a hawk—swooping in on the nests and grabbing the helpless babies in their jaws. When this happens, the sparrows go into a frenzy, flying around in circles, squawking madly. They freak out, but they can't fight back. The predators are too big. It happens every single year. I know it's the way of nature, but sometimes I want to call out to the sparrows, "Can't you guys get a strategy together for next season?"

It's clear to see that birds and animals are programmed to conform to the behaviors of their species. They have little choice about what they do or don't do in relationship to one another or the environment.

As human beings we have a phenomenal gift the sparrows don't have—consciousness. We aren't helpless to just sit by and watch events knock us off balance. We can stop and think, get clear on our priorities, reflect on our options, make a plan, choose a better way. Consciousness is not something we have to work for. We already have it. We only have to exercise it. Yet how often do we face stressful situations by flailing around helplessly just like the sparrows, instead of using our powers of awareness?

We often limit ourselves by going along with cultural conditioning coming from family, friends, and society. We pick up judgments about what is right or wrong, good or bad, and so on, without really thinking for ourselves. These judgments can interfere with our ability to see things as they are. The question is, how do we use our innate critical facilities in a productive, nonstressful way? Working for over thirty years with the Inner Game, I have focused on only three principles of learning. These principles are simple yet crucial to taking steps in your life. They are:

Awareness

Choice

Trust

Let's examine these principles. Each is part of a whole that allows for making desired changes, learning, and even unlearning.

Awareness

Awareness is one of the greatest tools of human consciousness. Like a light, it shines and makes things visible. By its nature it is nonjudgmental. It simply reveals what is going on in the here and now where life happens. It sees, feels, hears, and understands *what is* without distortion.

If you know where you are going, simply being aware of where you are will show you the next steps to take. For example, when I was coaching tennis, if a student was hitting the ball off center, in-

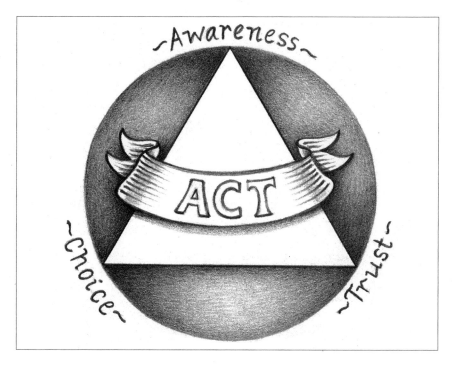

stead of analyzing why the ball was not hitting in the middle of the racquet I simply asked the player to be aware of where the ball was hitting the racquet without trying to make any change. Without the player's making any effort to control other than to be aware of where the ball hit the racquet, the balls would start clustering toward its center. Why? Awareness itself would inform Self 2 of what felt better, sounded better, and flew off the racquet better. Subtle adjustments were made by Self 2 in a very natural way.

Similarly, if I asked you right now to become more aware of how you are sitting while reading this page, it is likely that you would make subtle changes in your body's position if you felt anything that was less than comfortable.

The focusing of awareness is called attention. It allows you to become more aware of whatever is in the direction you are focusing. Where and how you place your attention makes a difference. In any situation, there are innumerable possible places to put your attention, but the best place to begin is with what I call the critical variables of that situation. I define a critical variable as anything that changes and that is crucial to your desired outcome. For example, in driving, your speed, position in the lane, and the proximity of other cars are a few of the obvious critical variables. Simply put, when you place your attention on the critical variables, you can move in synchronicity with your goal.

Not all critical variables are external. Some of the most powerful places for attention to be focused are within—for example, on your attitude, your hopefulness, your intentions, and your enjoyment. In fact, the doctors tell me that from a medical point of view, the critical variable of stress is the extent to which you are enjoying what you are doing at the time.

Focusing on critical variables benefits you in two important ways. First, it keeps your mind in the present and gives you information you need to move in your desired direction. Second, it doesn't leave room in your awareness for Self 1 interference about what might happen in the future or what has happened in the past. It's being able to just look and see something as it is without the criticism, the right and wrong, the good and bad, the should and could intruding. This is the first step in becoming free enough in your mind to develop wisdom. The secret is, if you want to change something, first increase your awareness of *the way it is.*

Once I was coaching Phil, an executive who had a reputation for being overly aggressive with those he was managing. It was as if everyone knew this but him. Feeling that Phil might be quite defensive if I confronted him directly about his behavior, I asked him the following question: "How can you tell when your staff members are really listening to what you tell them?"

"Well," he said, without thinking about it much, "I can tell by their eye contact with me, their body language, and finally, whether they comply with what I am asking of them."

"During the next week," I said, "I want you to just observe without judgment these variables in your staff when you are speaking with them. Then report to me what you notice at the end of the week." Phil went off, curious about his assignment. And he came back the next week as surprised as he was excited. "It was amazing," he said. "At the beginning of the week there was very little eye contact, and a lot of arms folded across their chests, and an apparent resistance to my directions. But by the end of the week, without me changing anything, they were quite different. Their eyes made contact, they looked like they were trying to absorb what I was saying, and they began producing results better and faster than I've ever seen them. Why do you think that is?"

"I'm not sure," I answered, "but here's your assignment for next week. Simply be aware of your tone of voice while you are speaking with your staff. Nonjudgmentally. Just listen."

The results are what you might now expect. Phil found that there was a significant change in his tone of voice and that he was establishing a much better connection with his people. Besides changing a sensitive behavior without stress, he learned the power of nonjudgmental awareness in the process. I imagine his staff was experiencing less stress at the same time.

PATIENT FILE

from John Horton, M.D.

PAIN IN THE GUT

A young man, Joe, came to see me, complaining of very bad stomach pains and bouts of nausea. Joe thought he might have an ulcer or even cancer. He was very worried. I did a thorough medical workup, and I couldn't find any specific cause. All the tests came out okay. So I referred Joe to a gastroenterologist; he did more studies, without detecting an illness.

I was reluctant to confront Joe about his stress levels because I knew he would take stress as a sign of weakness and not being good enough for the challenges of his young corporate life. He had told me his father was a tough, ambitious man, so he had a lot to live up to. He was newly married, and his wife wanted a family. He was not at all reflective, and wanted to run fast in his high-pressure career. Joe's family was trying to convince him to go to the Mayo Clinic, where the top experts might find some unusual disease to explain his stomach pains.

Sensing that Joe's symptoms were stress-related, I asked him if before resorting to a trip to the Mayo Clinic he would be willing to engage in a self-awareness exercise. I asked him to simply observe himself for a week, noting his pain and his behaviors just before the onset of the pain. He was to make these observations without any judgment, and see what he might discover. He agreed to do this.

The following week, Joe returned to my office, and he had a big smile on his face. He said, "Dr. Horton, my pain and nausea have been resolved about eighty percent."

I was impressed. "That's remarkable," I said. "What happened?"

Joe explained that he came home from work one day, very tired. As usual, he sat down cross-legged in front of the TV, put a book he was studying on the floor in front of him, and turned on the news. His wife handed him a plate of food, and he put that in front of him, too. As he ate, watched TV, and turned the pages of his book, he started to feel the familiar discomfort in his stomach. This time he made a point of thinking about what he was doing. He was bent over at nearly a ninety-degree angle, legs crossed in a pretzel-like position, eating, reading, and watching TV simultaneously. Without a word, he got up and moved his plate to the table and sat down across from his wife. For the first time in months they had a pleasant conversation over dinner, he digested his food easily, and the pain disappeared.

I laughed when he told me the story. "Had I known, I would have advised you at your first visit to stop eating your meals sitting cross-legged and bent over," I said. The remaining 20 percent of his symptoms were resolved when he noticed how nervous he felt before lunch meetings with his boss and other managers. He decided to eat well before or after the meetings.

Joe recalled that when he had told his boss he had chronic stomach pain, she had asked him if he was eating baby food yet. When he said that he wasn't, she replied, "Then you're not yet a serious corporate executive." For some people, having a stress-related illness is a badge of courage—a sign that they are willing to sacrifice for the cause.

I have had the pleasure of watching Joe weather the trials and tribulations of family and career with good health and enjoyment. When I last saw him he was managing a department of forty people in a downsizing situation in which everyone's workload was excessive. He was starting his own new business, and enjoying his family. When I asked him about any stress symptoms, he said forcefully, "I just don't do stress."

Exercise: Observing a Critical Variable

Choose one of the stressful situations you have identified in the prior exercises. Then pick an internal critical variable to observe such as attitude, intention, or enjoyment. During the next week, whenever you think of it, give this variable a score on a scale of one to ten, depending on how strongly it is present. Notice any changes that take place in your stress level as you do this exercise.

Choice

To be aware is itself a choice. You have the choice to shut your eyes, bury your head in the sand, and simply deny the truth about what is. Often this denial is based on judgment or fear. Nonjudgmental awareness gives you the power to look fear in the face and put it into proper perspective. Taking off the preconceived glasses of judgment, it is easier to see the reality of what is in front of you. This does not mean that the reality might not be tough to face, and that the confrontation might be shocking. But it is those kinds of shocks that we often learn the most from. It's simply our choice.

Conscious choice is there as soon as you realize you have it. The challenge is to *exercise* your conscious choice. The alternative strategy is to go through the day unaware of the choices you are making, where your choices are coming from, or their consequences.

Unconscious choices are hard to learn from. They just seem to happen, and we end up with their consequences often without being able to trace them to our own choices. Instead of learning to resolve problems as they come, we continue to invite the same problems again and again until we finally learn. In short, unconscious choices are destabilizing, while conscious choices add to our stability. The stability is like that of a large river whose source in the highlands begins with one drop (choice) at a time.

Health professionals are recognizing that personal responsibility is the key to preventing illness. A study by Ralph L. Keeney, a research professor at the Fuqua School of Business, found that personal decisions lead to about one million premature deaths in the United States annually. Although heart disease and cancer are widely considered the biggest killers, it is actually more accurate to blame the individual choices we make; behaviors such as smoking and unhealthy eating are frequently at the root of these diseases. Likewise, behaviors such as using drugs and driving recklessly contribute greatly to the number of annual preventable fatalities.

What do we base our choices on? That's one of our fundamental choices. Some say to base your choices on reasoning, and others say to base them on feeling or intuition. Many are unaware that choices come from desires that can be felt. If love is a feeling, then choices based on love can be felt. I also believe that the desires for excellence, peace, and contentment are inherent desires that can be felt and can inform our choices in life. These feel different from the desires of Self 1, which may just want something because someone else has it. You have the ability to distinguish the choices that come from your self-knowledge and intuition from those that come from your mental desires. This ability is a fundamental key to consciousness and human evolution. Stress interferes with the ability to make important distinctions. Fear focuses attention outward to the perceived danger, and you lose touch with your subtler needs and feelings.

For example, say it's Christmastime and you decide you want to get presents for those you love. You make a list of the people, buy the gifts, wrap them, and deliver them. As most of us know, it's all too easy to get so involved in completing the actions on your list that you forget the purpose that moved you to action in the first place. I often hear people complaining during the holidays about how harassed they are, how far removed they've become from the "Christmas spirit." However, when you stay connected with the feeling that gave purpose to the series of actions, it makes for a richer experience of those actions. Remembrance of your purpose on a day-to-day basis is a great stabilizer.

Knowing and remembering what you want in a way that is true to yourself allows a stable relationship with yourself. Obviously, you can think about what you want and its consequences for you and others, but to be able to feel clearly what you want is more profound than merely having a mental concept. Ignoring what you truly want in favor of pleasing others, or simply choosing what's convenient, weakens your stability.

Exercise: Desired Outcome

Return to your stressful situation and identify the unconscious choices that may have intensified your stress. Where did these choices come from?

Next, reflect on your desired outcome for this situation. Look for the feeling that this desire comes from and the conscious choice(s) you are willing to commit to. Put your commitment in writing.

Trust

The third side of the ACT triangle is trust. Actually, as with any triangle, there is not a first, second, and third side. Each side is interdependent on the other two. If you don't trust your capability to be aware or to make conscious choices, you'll be immobilized.

Awareness tells you where you are. Choice tells you where you want to be. A natural tension is created between the two. Trust in your own resources, inner and outer, is the key ingredient to movement toward your desired outcome.

Trust in itself cannot be considered a virtue. The virtue is to trust what is trustworthy. And how do you know what is trustworthy? Many will tell you what to trust, but in the final analysis you are left with your own wisdom. Paradoxically, you don't really have a choice about it. Even if you want to put your trust in another person, a book, or an idea, it is you who decides where to put your trust. When you place your trust in someone else or something else, you are still trusting yourself to decide who or what is trustworthy. You're stuck with *you* as the final choice maker in the matter.

But here's the key. If you trust Self 1, you'll get tied up in knots, because Self 1 is inherently untrustworthy. Trust in Self 2 and its inner abilities, on the other hand, is like magic. The more you trust it, the more trustworthy it becomes. Look at the trust children naturally put in themselves and their abilities to learn, to love, to enjoy. Without that trust, very little growing or evolving would happen.

When you get down to it, trusting Self 2 is the same as trusting life. Trusting ourselves is something we do intuitively and naturally. We trust more than we realize. We trust our hearts to beat and our lungs to breathe. If we worried about every heartbeat, or weren't confident that our next breath was coming, we'd be frozen. But we have an innate ability, without trying, to trust that we will function well unless something gets in the way.

This is probably the most difficult thing to understand—that we can actually trust ourselves to function productively and successfully, to intuitively know how to be what and who we are.

Let's take it a step further. Can you trust that life can be lived well—that it's not out to get you? When you are focused on the "good" that life is bringing your way, you worry less about the "bad," and you can walk more easily.

I once did a consult for Matt, a businessman who was at a very precarious place in his business. Matt told me, "I'm used to handling large amounts of stress," but this time he was in a bind. He'd invested a lot of money in a start-up company, and so far he didn't have a single customer. He was angry, frustrated, and ashamed. His self-confidence had really suffered a blow, and he said, "I feel like a failure."

Matt was looking for business strategies to make a change in his situation. I couldn't give him a surefire solution. Maybe the business would work, maybe it wouldn't. I saw that the primary thing he had to do was to separate his self-worth from the outcome. And while he was making the effort, he had two choices. He could worry that the outcome was a measure of his self-worth, or he could trust. Trust what? Trust his proven abilities to live and be productive. Effort plus trust in himself would put him in the best position possible to succeed. Anger, self-doubt, and confusion would interfere. He saw it was that simple.

PATIENT FILE

from John Horton, M.D.

TRUST THE MESSENGER

Mary, a patient with multiple sclerosis, was having a hard time recovering from a viral illness. She was anticipating traveling in the coming weeks to an important conference, and was extremely distraught that she couldn't shake her flu. The rest of her family had also been sick, but they had easily recovered. Not Mary. In fact, each day she grew progressively worse, sweating profusely each time she exerted herself. I told Mary that people with MS have greater difficulty recovering from illnesses, and that she needed to rest. This opened up a remarkable conversation.

Mary told me that she had an abhorrence of "just sitting and doing nothing." When she was a child, she had seen her mother depressed and immobile, and she associated inactivity with her mother's depression. Although Mary had MS, she was an incredibly energetic woman, who constantly pushed herself. "I have no clue how to rest," she admitted.

"Can you trust your body?" I asked. "You see rest as a negative, but your body is telling you that it would be quite productive right now for you to do nothing."

This understanding was an incredible breakthrough for Mary. Once she accepted the felt need to rest, she began to recover quickly. In the process she found that she was delighted by the sheer pleasure of doing nothing. For Mary, it was almost a religious experience. In short, she had learned to trust her own experience of her body's wisdom rather than her fear of being immobilized by depression like her mother.

Once you trust that you possess the inner resources to overcome stress, that trust becomes the foundation of your stability.

Exercise: Trusting

Consider a stressful circumstance, and make a list of what you trust in the situation. Reflect on whether it is worthy of trust, or leaves you feeling uncertain and unstable. Is your trust based on your own experience or on a concept you were taught?

SEVEN

Your Tree of Stability

STABILITY IS THAT WHICH RESISTS BEING TOPPLED. IT IS NOT THE outside force; it is the inner resilience. Imagine two trees in the presence of gale-force winds. One is a palm tree on the beach, whose flexible trunk allows it to sway with the wind but not be broken. In a ferocious storm, it might be laid practically flat to the sand, but when the wind disperses, it stands back up. Another tree, perhaps an inland oak, with a rigid trunk, will snap in two in a heavy wind. What is the difference between the fates of the two trees? It is not the amount of wind. It is the stability of the roots and the flexibility of the trunk and branches. We too need stability and flexibility in facing the winds of change and loss.

One goal of the Inner Game is to build foundational stability. To use a simple example, consider the children's story of the three little pigs. The first little pig built his house out of straw because it was the easiest thing to do. The second little pig built his house out of sticks—somewhat stronger than a straw house. The third little pig built his house out of bricks. One night the big bad wolf came along. He blew down the house made of straw, and he ate the first little pig. Then he blew down the house made of sticks, and he ate the second little pig. But when he came to the house of bricks, he was unable to blow it down. The question isn't what you do in the moment of stress, when it's already too late to protect yourself. It's how you build inner stability so that you're protected whenever the wolf blows at the door of your house.

The following exercise is designed to help you understand your own stability. It will be valuable for you to do this now, before reading further into this chapter.

Exercise: Your Tree of Stability

The Tree of Stability exercise is a powerful way to become aware of how strong and deep your roots are, and to get a picture of your current level of stability. As you make changes in your life, you may want to do the exercise again to see your progress.

1. Use the tree on page 91 or draw yourself a tree with its trunk in the middle of the page. Include roots of various thickness and depth.

2. Label each root with an aspect of your life that contributes to your stability. To help identify your roots, you can ask yourself, "Without this would I be less stable?" Let the depth and thickness of the root reflect its importance. Make this a spontaneous activity. There's no need to analyze at first.

3. Above the tree, draw elements that can shake or threaten it—such as rain, lightning, wind—and label each of these with one of the major stressors in your life that can threaten your stability. In additon to external stressors, you can include the inner voice of the Stress Maker.

4. Make a general assessment of the overall strength of your
   tree. Ask yourself, how much would it take right now to
   compromise its stability? What would be the minimum
   event that would actually topple that tree? If the minimum
   would be a tornado touching down in your back yard, I'd say

your tree is pretty stable. But if you're at a point where the minimum is a minor windstorm, you are close to the edge and need some stronger roots.

5. Sit back and reflect on your tree's roots of stability. See if you have any observations or insights. It is not unusual for people to realize that they have listed the same things as both roots of stability and as major stressors. For example, your job may be an important aspect of your stability, providing income and perhaps meaning, but the same job can also be a major source of stress. In fact, the threat of being laid off, with the loss of that root, can be a constant worry. Similarly, if one of your roots is physical health, how shaky would your tree become if you got a serious medical diagnosis? Family can also provide great stability, and at the same time become a source of stress. We all rely on our loved ones, our work, and our health to keep us strong. That's natural. But they introduce instability into our tree, because if they are threatened, foundations are shaken.

Another way to look at your roots is to consider whether they are external or internal. A child can move away, a career can change course, a marriage can falter, a parent can die. If you rely on any of these for stability, you are constantly in danger of being toppled by events that are outside your control. Usually, when people first do this Tree of Stability exercise in our seminars, almost all of the roots they name are external. By the end of the seminar, they have come to value the stability of internal roots.

In our stress seminars, when people reflect on their Tree of Stability, they can have very different insights. In a recent workshop, one participant said, "If I don't get more roots soon, my tree is going to topple over." Another said after the workshop, "I was surprised at how many roots I had. Now, whenever I feel stress I remember all the roots of stability I have in my tree and I immediately start to feel stronger."

This commonsense exercise has helped a lot of people clarify the difference between the Inner Game and the Outer Game, and to appreciate the effect this distinction can have on their stability.

PATIENT FILE

---

from Edd Hanzelik, M.D.

UNSHAKABLE SPIRITS

After the Northridge, California, earthquake in January 1994, I would see patients who were right in the middle of it. Their houses were destroyed and they experienced tremendous upheaval, and yet they were calm. They were glad to be alive. They were grateful. They busied themselves finding new places to live. They were not at all shaken. And then there were other people who couldn't sleep. They couldn't breathe normally. They bordered on being hysterical. They needed psychotherapy. These symptoms often continued for months and months. The earthquake hit us all, but some of us got thrown profoundly away from our inner stability. And others were rooted more deeply.

NOTICE YOUR INNER RESOURCES

The point is, you have to ground your stability in the things that are stable. For example, you're breathing. Isn't that the first root of stability? Breathing is reliable. If you're reading this, you probably haven't missed too many breaths in your life.

Inner resources are just there. Maybe you don't know you have them, but it doesn't mean they don't exist. To use an analogy, imagine that you bought a big piece of property, and somewhere on your land is an orange grove, and on another part of your land is an avocado grove. But you never see them, because you never stray more than thirty feet from your front door. The groves are there, you just haven't explored your property and seen them.

Another way to look at it is to view inner resources as your hardware, and your thinking as the software. The hardware keeps the machine running. Software can be changed.

Earlier we talked about how you can identify true inner resources by using three measures:

1. They are qualities that are found in children.
2. We admire these qualities when we see them in others.
3. We like these qualities when we see them in ourselves.

Simply put, if we notice these attributes in small children, we can be pretty confident that they're natural, since children haven't yet added on all the layers of software. If we admire these qualities in others, we can be assured that they're possible for us as well, because they are part of the human hardware. And if we like them in ourselves, we can acknowledge that what we enjoy will also make us stronger.

Exercise: Your Inner Resources

Make a list of the qualities and abilities that you consider to be inner resources. In your selection process use the three measures above. Spend a few minutes making your own list before referring to the list below from our seminar participants.

Clarity	*Joy*
Imagination	*Peacefulness*
Humor	*Wonder*
Intuition	*Intelligence*
Creativity	*Compassion*

Hope	Empathy
Appreciation	Commitment
Courage	Kindness
Love	Spontaneity
Understanding	Enthusiasm
Choice	Trust
Humility	Sincerity
Learning	Awe

Look again at the roots you labeled on your Tree of Stability and notice if they are mostly internal or external. We discussed earlier how external roots can also be turned into threats. Basing your stability on your inner resources, which can grow without limit, makes you much stronger.

To possess any one of these qualities is admirable, but you actually have all of them, built-in and ready to use. The inner resources are your stabilizing hardware—always available, no matter what happens. If, for example, one of the roots of your tree is *hope*, it will help you stay strong when things aren't going your way. *Humor* can be healing; there is much medical evidence to that effect. *Compassion* can turn resentment into openness. And so on.

The inner resources are like a collection of precious gifts, all packed in a handsome suitcase. To most fully enjoy the journey of life, you will need to unpack the suitcase and utilize its contents.

PATENT FILE

from John Horton, M.D.

PLEASING ONESELF

Cheryl was diagnosed with cancer, and over the period of a year, she needed major surgery and several courses of chemotherapy. Cheryl and her husband came in for coaching sessions to help handle all of the difficulties of this time. Cheryl did extraordinarily well.

One day we were recognizing how well she was doing, and I asked her, "So what is your secret?" Cheryl reflected for a moment, and responded innocently, "I am pleased to please myself." It was a wonderful observation—one that stuck with me. Cheryl's husband laughingly admitted that he was actually a little bit envious that his wife was able to enjoy herself in the shadow of such a serious illness.

Cheryl's cancer was eventually cured—or as close to it as doctors could determine. A few years later, her husband died suddenly. She coped well with this new crisis, and once again, I admired the inner stability she had built up over time.

Coincidentally, Cheryl called with a minor problem while I was working on the book. I asked her if she was still pleased to be pleasing herself. She replied, "Yes, definitely." She was still experiencing the loss of her husband, but felt that the next chapter of her life would be in Europe with her son. Her inner calm and clarity were striking. I asked her what she thought the purpose of life was. She said, "To enjoy it," and added that most people postpone that.

I was happy to hear of the continuity of her commitment. Was the idea of being "pleased to please myself" selfish or wise? Cheryl's choice certainly helped to save her life, and to enjoy her time on earth. Her ability to be pleased with herself and her life, in the face of great illness and loss, is certainly the foundation of wisdom.

Exercise: Acknowledge Your Stability

Pick two or three of your inner resources, and consider how you can use them right now in the face of a particular stressor.

When your stability is deep and strong, the challenges of life don't shake you as much. You can step back, reflect, accept, access your inner wisdom, and develop a strategy on how to proceed. We see this in the survivors of horrible diseases or major catastrophes. We see it in some Holocaust survivors. Yet the capacity for stability isn't just present in these amazing people. It's available to everyone.

EIGHT

Build a Personal Shield

You can protect your stability by building a personal shield. The shield can be made out of inner abilities of your own choosing. The last one I made for myself consisted of five inner resources that I thought would best protect me—clarity, hope, understanding, awareness, and courage.

I can change what I put on my shield at any time depending on what I feel would be most valuable to protect me.

Besides the shield, I choose to wear the soft but powerful armor of understanding, and carry a sharp, bright, lightweight sword of clarity that can cut through any confusion, doubt, or foolish concept. I usually keep these two in place as they are always necessary. In their practice, John and Edd witness every day how powerful such shields can be for people with life-threatening and terminal illnesses, and how much better they work than other psychological defenses or medications.

Recently, I participated in a remarkable filmed dialogue with

Pete Carroll, the head football coach of USC. I'm sure Pete will go down in history as one of the greatest. And he is definitely a man who uses personal shields in the extremely high-pressured environment of competitive college football.

I knew Pete had read *The Inner Game of Tennis* in his early years as a coach, so I was interested in seeing if and how he applied what he understood to coaching football. When he invited me to do the dialogue, he said he had applied his understanding of the Inner Game to his fundamental approach to coaching. He humbly said that one thing he wanted to discover was whether he had gotten it right. I found, as we spoke, that he used the Inner Game in all aspects of his personal life as well.

The meeting took place at Heritage Hall, which is the inner sanctum of USC football. There was a small group of about fifty invited guests.

One of the questions I asked Pete was how he dealt with the most stressful moments in a football game. His answer was spontaneous and intriguing to me. First, he said that he welcomed and appreciated those moments above all others, because they brought out the best of his and his team's inner resources. He said that there were only three or four moments like that in a game, and he looked forward to each of them. He spoke with such innocence and confidence that he was immediately credible.

Another insight Pete shared was that he had created a great deal of inner stability by working with his team to develop contingency plans for the critical moments. He said, "It's all about contingencies." He noted that once he had drilled his team in practice on each of the contingencies that might face them, he was able to say, "We have been here before. We know what to do."

I was impressed with Pete's ability to accept any situation and see it as an opportunity. It is challenging for many people to accept, much less prepare for, the possible contingencies they face. They prefer to live in denial, which makes them very vulnerable to stress when unexpected things do happen. But having workable contingency plans is a very practical way to build stability.

Pete told me how necessary it was that he have a personal shield that protected him from the opinions of the players, fans, and alumni. He listened to their opinions, but he knew he had to reach his own judgments. He was the CEO, able to freely decide.

Perhaps the most remarkable thing I saw in Pete Carroll was his alertness to any negative thinking or doubt. His motto was "Win Forever!" But these were not just words for him. In conversations, thoughts and actions, he left no room for Self 1 fears and uncertainties to enter his mind. He built his shield on the practice field, and he used it in every conversation about football and coaching he had with anyone. The rare defeats he sustained he felt deeply, but bounced back immediately into the stability of his philosophy and practice. He has developed a shield against stress.

We usually have unconscious psychological defenses to protect ourselves, but they generally develop without our awareness when we are young, and they frequently become restricting and burdensome. Building your own Personal Shield is a chance to create a conscious, effective defense, which you can use to protect yourself from stressors.

Exercise: Build Your Shield

Consider a stressful situation you are facing right now. Go to your list of inner resources and choose four or five that could be constructed into a shield when you are in the midst of the situation. Draw a shield like the one on page 99 and carry it with you as a reminder.

LEARNING TO CHANGE DESTABILIZING HABITS

Building your personal shield has a lot to do with changing unconscious habits. We all have our ways of changing, and it can be said we are constantly changing, like it or not. But conscious change is more powerful.

I remember that when I was a little kid, I was a thumb sucker. And when I was five, I decided I was going to stop sucking my thumb. My older sister said, "Thumb sucking can be really hard to change. It's been a habit for a long time." I looked at her and said, "Why should it be hard? It's *my* hand. *My* thumb. And I put it into *my* mouth. So I can take it out of *my* mouth if I want." So I stopped sucking my thumb.

I wish I could have kept that simple understanding and courage. It's very possible, when you think about it: You want to change? So change. It's your hand.

Most habits have a reason for being formed in the first place. That reason may no longer apply for you, but it was there once. So before you set about changing a habit, it's a good idea to check out where the habit came from, what purpose it served, and if it is still serving you in the best way. Here's an approach I use: Once I've determined that I want to make a change, the first thing I have to do is grant myself mobility. Mobility is the ability to move toward your desired outcome. When people talk about being trapped by a bad habit, they complain, "It's just too hard to change." But is that really true? Perhaps it's hard to break a deeply ingrained habit; it can be like digging your way out of a ditch. But an alternative strategy, which works well, is to leave the old habit and start a new one. In other words, focus on what you want to be doing, instead of what feels wrong. This perspective has the same effect as a shield. It doesn't require you to undo what's wrong, just to do what feels right.

The first time I learned this—profoundly—I was coaching Joe, the CEO of a large company, in tennis. He announced at the start that he wanted to change the bad habit he had with his backhand.

"On my backswing, I think my racquet is too high," he stated, before even going to the court. "I put backspin on the ball, and it tends to float out."

I was curious. "How do you know your racquet is too high?" I asked him.

"Well," he replied, "the last twelve pros I've been to have all told me the same thing." I almost couldn't believe my ears. He'd been to twelve pros, and I was number thirteen. Not a very auspicious beginning!

I asked him to take a swing where we were standing. He did, and I saw that the twelve pros were correct. He had accurately described his problem. But I was thinking, "If twelve people have told him the problem, and he's still doing it, how am I going to be successful?"

We were standing on the patio of the club, and my eyes drifted toward the dining room. There was a plateglass window, floor to ceiling, and in the light of the afternoon, it gave off reflections, like a mirror. I said, "Joe, would you go over to the window and take a swing?"

He looked at me a little puzzled, but he did it. He took a swing, staring at his reflection. Then he took another. On the third swing, he said with surprise, "Oh, my God, it's true. I *do* take my racquet too high."

Now, how can a person be surprised at finding out something he already knows? Joe himself had told me, "My racquet is too high." Twelve pros had told him his racquet was too high. Yet here he was, surprised to see it for himself.

Joe knew what his problem was, but he had never actually been directly aware of it for himself. I don't call that *knowing*. I call it *believing*. He believed what he had been told, but it wasn't real for him until he saw it for himself.

So, now that Joe recognized his bad habit, how could he change it? We went down to the tennis court, and I started throwing balls to him. "Don't try to change it right now," I instructed. "Just notice it as it is—not by looking, but by feeling. Feel the level."

He swung, and said, "That seemed to be head high."

I said, "Right."

"You mean that's what I should do?" he asked.

I said, "No. That's what you just did. Don't try to change it. Just keep feeling it, and reporting its height to me."

I could see this seemed like a strange instruction to Joe. How could just being aware change anything for the better? But he accepted it, and kept swinging at balls and reporting his racquet level. When he started, his racquet was head high, then shoulder high, then head high, then it varied between chest high and waist high for a few balls, then below the waist. And pretty soon, all of his swings were low, and he was hitting topspin backhands.

I asked Joe, "Are you trying to take your racquet low?"

"No," he said, "it's doing it by itself."

Obviously, racquets don't swing by themselves. But Joe was not making a conscious effort to force it to be low. He was simply making a conscious effort to observe where it was. What took it lower was that it *felt* better and worked better. A new habit was forming. This new habit was not the result of Joe trying to force his racquet down, but the awareness of his racquet's level. Acknowledging this, Joe reflected on how it was an easy way to change a habit. "This could make a big difference at my company," he said. "But the best thing is that I can finally hit topspin backhands after all these years!"

The point is, we can all learn to change mental or physical habits without stress. The key is awareness. Not awareness that you have the habit, but awareness of the behavior itself. It's a matter of observation and knowing what you want. If you start with the premise, "This is bad, I have to change it," you're immediately in fight-or-flight mode. Take away the judgment, and you'll be amazed at what you actually see, and the ease with which change can take place.

PATIENT FILE

from Edd Hanzelik, M.D.

A SAMURAI APPROACH TO HEALTH

Debbie was a markedly stressed patient. She couldn't live in her house due to a major flood. A fire broke out in the hotel she was staying in and she had to abruptly leave there as well. She was exhausted and financially challenged.

The stress was already having a major effect on Debbie's health. She had lost her voice, probably from screaming out in despair. She wasn't able to scream anymore—in fact, she could barely speak above a whisper. A specialist had told her she might have laryngitis for months.

Seeing that Debbie viewed her daily life as a battle, I asked her, "Do you suppose you could be like a samurai warrior, and maintain your stability in the midst of the battle?"

Debbie looked doubtful. "Would I have to stuff all my feelings inside me?" she asked.

I replied, "No, that would not work. That would wreck your body. You need to channel your feelings into constructive actions."

I then asked Debbie whether she could see any benefit in not being able to speak. "If you went on a Zen retreat, it would cost you a few hundred dollars, and the first rule would be No Speaking," I said. "You're getting the same opportunity for free!"

She laughed at this remark and seemed to lighten in her attitude. She had been in the habit of feeling sorry for herself, but seemed open to looking at her situation another way.

Instead of feeling pity for her, I gave her a challenge. "Is there any way that none of these stressful circumstances would actually get to you?" Again, I asked if she could be the samurai in the center of the battle. This image of herself made her laugh. She said she would need a lot of courage, strength, and clarity in her personal shield. She felt she had to do it, and left smiling, telling me, "I still have my sense of humor."

"Add that to your personal shield," I recommended.

Debbie was experiencing an intense kind of stress in which everything in life appears to be going against you. The Stress Maker has a field day in this kind of stress, imagining the worst possible outcomes, such as homelessness, poverty, and even death. When Debbie started to build a personal shield to protect herself from her many stressors, and took advantage of her access to inner resources, including humor, determination, and trust, she discovered she still had some stability in the midst of the battle. She was indeed a samurai. On subsequent visits, she saw that she was gradually improving, and was able to reduce her experience of stress.

Exercise: Create a New Habit

Think about a habit you are struggling with. It can be any activity that is getting in the way of your productivity, health, or peace of mind. It will probably be something you have tried to stop doing in the past. What new habit can you create to replace the old one? For example, if you smoke, a new habit might be an activity that focuses on clear and strong breathing—something incompatible with smoking. Instead of trying to break the old habit, institute the new one.

For example, Doctor Horton told me how he stopped smoking in medical school. He read a study by psychoanalysts showing that some people smoked in order to step back from situations where they were feeling overwhelmed. Doctor Horton recognized himself in this description, and decided to consciously make an effort to step back and think about what was happening rather than light a cigarette. His smoking habit was broken quickly with this insight.

It is true that once you come to a deep understanding of the reasons you have a habit you want to change, and you are truly attracted to the new behavior, the process can be simple and short. Realistically, it can take some time, awareness, and reflection to come to this point.

THE ABILITY TO SAY "NO!"
AND MEAN IT

It's clear that a lot of things in our everyday life can be very stressful. They come at us randomly, and they can come from the people closest to us—those who make us happy or unhappy, who make demands on us that we would rather not accept.

One of the components of a shield that can protect you from such stressors is the ability to say no. When you drive a car, you have brakes as well as an accelerator. The ability to say no is your brake. We have to humbly recognize our limitations. Recently, I noticed a sign behind the cash register of a local deli that read:

Dear Judith,
Do not feel totally
Personally, irrevocably
Responsible for
Everything.
That's my job.
Love,
God

Being able to say no is part of the recognition that your stability and enjoyment have value. If you automatically say yes to everything that comes along, you will gradually undermine your ability to function well.

Being creative in the face of demands is the job of your accelerator, which can involve delegation, contingency planning, and respecting your real priorities in life. Obviously, a balance that keeps your vehicle stable and running in good condition is the number one priority.

Imagine that you're the owner of a property, and for years people made it a practice to walk across your lawn to get to the train station, because it was the quickest route for them. After just accepting it for a long time, you finally say, "Wait a minute. This is my property, and I don't want people walking on my lawn." So you build a fence around your yard, kind of like a shield. At first, the people who were used to walking there get annoyed at you for cutting off their access. But soon they find other routes, and your property is protected. You've essentially created a shield of protection. You can do the same thing in everyday life.

Exercise: Just Say No

For one week, be conscious of all of the requests that are made of you by others. Write them down and make a list. At the end of the week, review the list. How many times did you agree to things that increased your stress? Were there occasions when you could have declined but didn't? How have these observations changed your perspective as you enter a new week?

NINE

Be the CEO of Your Life

Inner stability rests on the acknowledgment of one indisputable fact: Your life is yours. You are its owner. Ownership is the foundation of stability and responsibility. You are the chooser. You are a sovereign. You have the rights and the responsibilities of ownership of something very incredible—a unique human body and a unique human life. If you don't acknowledge the ownership of your life, it's difficult if not impossible to build a lasting stability.

My friend Leslye had a ninety-four-year-old uncle who came to live with her. Over breakfast one morning, she asked him, "Uncle Jaime, have you enjoyed your life? You're getting on in years, and probably don't have many left. I just wondered if you enjoyed it."

Uncle Jaime stopped eating and thought for a moment. Then he said soberly, "No, I didn't."

Leslye was taken aback. She hadn't expected that. She said, "Uncle Jaime—why not?"

His answer was thoughtful. "You know, I gave it all away," he said. "I gave it to my wife, my kids, my church, my job . . ." and he kept listing things.

Her uncle's words had a huge impact on Leslye. She wanted to own her life.

So, how do you know if you're in charge of yourself or not? How much of what you do is based on pleasing other people? When you're in control, you know you're driving the car. Your hands are firmly on the steering wheel, and you're going where you want to go. Your foot is on the accelerator, and when you want to stop, you switch to the brake. It's simple and mostly instinctive. But let's say your car is filled with backseat drivers who assume they have a right to determine the direction of the car, shouting, "Slow down . . . turn here . . . go right . . . go left." These people are talking as if they have some control of the steering wheel, even though they clearly don't. Your choice is whether to cede control.

An acquaintance of mine once asked me if I thought he should call a certain woman for a date. He was very unsure about it, and I had the feeling that he would let my answer influence him a lot. So I said, "Let me ask you something. If you were driving a car, would you prefer to drive from the front seat, with your hands on the steering wheel, or from the backseat?" And he said, "That's easy. I'd be in the backseat."

I was surprised. "Really?" I asked. "You'd rather be in the backseat with nobody at the wheel?" He assured me that he would rather be in the backseat. When I asked why, he said, "Because either way, whether I was at the wheel or in the backseat, I'd probably get into an accident, but if I were in the backseat, it wouldn't be my fault!" Glimpsing the absurdity of his statement, he smiled, said thank you, and walked off.

It's a funny story, but a lot of people are like that. They avoid sitting in the driver's seat of their own car. They prefer to say, "I didn't choose this. It isn't my fault." But when it's your life, that's a pretty serious decision to make. Who wants to have it written on their tombstone, "It wasn't my fault"?

The choice to be in charge of your life and not be a victim is probably the most important factor in building inner stability.

This choice can be made again and again, when you need to reset your attitude.

ARE YOU THE CEO OF YOUR LIFE?

Imagine that you've inherited a medium-sized corporation from a rich uncle, and instantly you're in charge. You're the CEO and sole owner. Sitting in your seat at the head of the table, you can ask any questions and make any decisions you want. You have vice presidents and consultants you can listen to, but it's not a democracy. You are the only one who decides how choices will be made. That's what ownership means.

From this foundation of ownership you begin to think like a CEO of your own corporation. The difference is simply your realization that you have the authority to make changes in whatever you don't like about the company. One of the decisions you get to make as the head of the corporation is whether and to whom you'll sell shares. When you sell shares, you cede bits of ownership. This is okay in a corporation. But now, let's say this corporation you own is *you*.

The first task is to make a clear and conscious decision about your mission, values, product, strategies, and partnerships—as you would if you were the CEO of a company. These are building blocks of stability.

Second, consider the matter of your company's stock. You aren't required to sell shares of ownership to anyone. In fact, independence decreases to the extent that you've sold shares to others—they now have voting powers in your decisions. Many of us have sold enough shares that we have become minority shareholders in our own lives. The more shares you have sold, the less control you have, and the more likely you are to experience stress.

"A house divided against itself cannot stand," Abraham Lincoln said. That rings true to me when I think about the house of my own life.

Fortunately, you can "buy back" the shares you've sold, once you identify who now owns them and the price you sold them for.

For example, shares are often sold to others for love, approval, respect, or security. When buying back shares, you may risk losing what you sold them for. Of course, when two or more people, acting as sovereign entities, make conscious agreements, such as to say yes or no to a request, to form a team or a company or to get married, shares are not necessarily sold. Agreements can be made between sovereign entities; both retain their full sovereignty.

So, if you have sold shares in your life, the question becomes are you willing to buy them back, even if it means risking the commodity you sold them for? It just may be the price of stability.

PATIENT FILE

from Edd Hanzelik, M.D.

WHOSE LIFE IS IT?

Karen developed a lump in her breast, which was biopsied and found to be cancerous. She was scheduled for surgery, and she had some strong opinions about the way she wanted it done. Now, this in itself is remarkable. Most often, when patients face a life-threatening diagnosis, they feel small and helpless. They just say, "All right, doctor, whatever you say."

But Karen was determined to hold her ground and negotiate for all the things she felt were important. And she had an appealing way of doing it that tended to win people over. One of those things was that in the recovery room after surgery, Karen wanted an infusion of megadose vitamins. In the world of medical care, this was complete heresy. But that's what she wanted. So I gave her a list of some of the vitamins that could be in the infusion, and she took it to her surgeon. And she did it in a playful enough way that he agreed to take care of it for her.

I attended Karen's surgery, and she gave me a list of my responsibilities—to make sure she got the vitamins, to check out the dye that was being used, to ensure that her headphones were playing what she wanted to be listening to, and so on. And everything went smoothly, including the vitamins. Why? Because Karen had won over the surgeon, and he said, "She's a little out there, but she's really nice, and I promised her these vitamins." And with that declaration, the anesthesiologist and the pharmacist fell into line.

When it came to chemotherapy, Karen was determined to partake on her own terms. Wanting to feel strong, she chose clothes that would give her that feeling, a red cape and a striking hat. The oncologist didn't know what to make of it, but he could see her outfit was helping her accept and go through the treatment.

Karen took ownership of her body and her medical care and stood up for herself. By doing this, she turned a very difficult situation into something she could accept.

How many times have you gone to the doctor, and found events happening before you had a chance to think about it? Doctors are trained to fight disease, and sometimes they take that clinical view. A doctor will say, "I had an interesting heart attack today." Or "I treated a lung infection." They're fighting the enemy—disease—and they have a full array of weapons— knives, radiation, medication.

But where does the patient come in—the individual? A lot of patients, who try to be heard or ask questions, get a response that amounts to, "Stay out of the way. Let me fight this battle, and I'll let you know when it's over."

Most people have bought into this idea of compliance and passivity. You'll hear people say things like, "The doctor said I had to have a heart operation," as if that ended all discussion. It's like an almighty being has spoken, and the patient has no choice. And yet, when it's your life on the line, that's when you need choice more than ever.

In my experience—and this finding has been supported by medical studies—the more actively patients participate in their own care, the better the doctors' decisions and the better the outcomes. Diabetes is a perfect example. When patients accept that they have this condition and choose to do something about it, they can get excellent control of their blood sugar and often are able to reduce or stop medications.

YOUR OWNER'S MANUAL

Taking ownership of your life means being truly independent—thinking for yourself, living with no strings attached, and being able to have rich relationships without losing yourself. There are many ways to describe this state of existence, but for sure it means that you are able to make the profound decisions for your life freely.

When you lack independence, you will find yourself doing things out of a sense of "I have to" rather than "I want to" or "I choose to." Your overriding experience can be one of helplessness, that you are a victim of circumstances or of other people's expectations. Being a victim doesn't feel good, and it doesn't really work.

Fortunately, there's a choice. If you choose to accept responsibility for ownership of your life, you can buy back outstanding shares, achieve your goals, and enjoy the entire process. People wonder how they can recoup shares if they're married, or have a family, or have business partners. Can they really be independent? In my experience, it is possible to have these relationships with integrity, without giving up ownership of your life. You want the relationship to work, so you choose to resolve differences. That is not the same as feeling forced to do things that do not feel good to you, because you have sold shares. Two independent owners can choose to get married and enjoy their lives together. How different that is from a marriage in which one of the partners is obsessed with needing to feel more accepted by his spouse. Unconsciously, he gives up participating in decisions in his efforts to be more accepted. By compromising his independence, he weakens the relationship.

The key to healthy relationships is a state of what might be called interdependence—two or more healthy, independent selves coming together to achieve common goals without sacrificing their individual integrity.

We all know the frustration and fear that come from having lost ourselves in relationships to family, friends, spouses, children, or even pets. This will activate the stress system and you may find yourself unconsciously living in fight, flight, or freeze reactions. Becoming conscious of these reactions can give you clues about where you have compromised your independence. For example, notice if you become stressed in conversations at work or in relationships at home, or with certain friends. These are hints about where you have sold shares.

You can also lose independence when you find yourself living with ideas, concepts, ideologies, and biases that are not aligned with your feelings and values. Consider what happens when human beings lose a sense of their basic values and get swept away in blind violence and destruction. The wisest leaders exhort us to prize our personal individual independence and shared human values.

SITTING IN THE CEO'S CHAIR

When I am the CEO in the chair, there is a feeling of profound humility—an appreciation of how much I have been given as a human being: my very life, as well as all my innate human abilities; the ability to set a purpose and move toward it; the ability to be aware; the ability to know what I really want, what is most precious to me, and what my priorities are.

I can learn from my choices and from the choices of others. I have the power to appreciate and feel grateful, joyful, and content. These are all within my capabilities as CEO. And at any point in time, I can decide to make changes with wisdom and clarity. Whenever I lose the sense of being CEO—abdicating responsibility to someone or something else—I can reclaim the position by a declaration of the obvious: I am in charge of my life.

This does not mean I can't take advice or guidance from others. Quite the opposite. I can listen and learn, and use what makes sense to me. But I am the final decider. That is the responsibility of the CEO—to be conscious and to discover and use the capabilities I have been given.

THE INNER GAME TOOLBOX

In the next section, we'll provide Inner Game tools that will offer practical steps you can take to build and maintain stability, to create effective personal shields, to gain access to your body's natural wisdom, and to become the CEO of your life. We have used all of these tools in our stress seminars for many years, and we have seen how valuable they can be. The tools are simple to understand. Go through each exercise as you read the chapters, and then practice using the tools in your everyday life. You will see how you can greatly reduce the stress you are experiencing.

PART THREE

THE INNER GAME
TOOLBOX

TEN

Inner Game Tool #1:
STOP

STRESS HAS A MOMENTUM ALL ITS OWN, LIKE A BILLIARD BALL AFTER it's struck by another ball. Many people, when they are stressed, become like billiard balls. They're slammed and they move—not in an intentional direction, but wherever the impact takes them. When you ask them why they did something self-destructive, they'll say, "Because I had a lousy day at work," or "My wife and I had a fight." Being a billiard ball is pretty stressful! Life becomes a matter of waiting for the next ball to hit you and drive you into a hole. But what if you were stable enough that when you got hit you didn't move? What if you only moved when *you* decided to, not when an external force hit you?

If you play golf, you may have experienced this negative momentum. Early in the game you hit a bad shot and the ball is gone, rolling into the woods. You start thinking, "Oh, that does it. What a lousy shot. The game is ruined. I'm not playing well today, what a bummer." And so on. At that point, you might as well pack up your clubs and go home. Recovery of your outer game is unlikely if your inner game is already lost. But what if instead you took a couple of seconds to ask, "Why am I playing today? What's my goal here?" Sure, you want to hit the ball into the hole. But what's the real goal? To have fun, enjoy yourself. Are you enjoying yourself if you're beating yourself up over a lost shot? Probably not.

An intelligent, fit marathon runner in his sixties came to the stress seminar because he'd been having such severe anxiety attacks that he had to be hospitalized for a few days. He realized, "I was so busy being busy that I didn't have time to stop." His inability to step back from the momentum of his life was ruining his health.

How do you halt negative momentum? By literally stopping.

THE SIMPLICITY OF STOP

In thirty-five years of coaching athletes, business professionals, and others, I have found the most effective technique to be the STOP tool. Thousands of managers from companies around the world have told me it is indispensable for being conscious at work. It can be called the mother of all tools because without stopping you can't really use any of the other tools. In our stress seminars, it is the first one we teach. Everyone understands it and recognizes its wisdom, because most people have used a variation of it. Parents talk about giving their children a "timeout." Others recall being told to "count to ten" before they act. Most sports teams use timeouts not only to rest but to think about changes in strategy or tactics.

STOP is a surprisingly simple tool, and it means exactly what it says: Stop the unconscious momentum and make the shift to being conscious. This tool is comprised of four parts:

Step back. Put some distance between you and the situation.

Think. What is the truth about what is happening? What's

causing you to feel stress in this situation? What are your priorities? Your options? Your obstacles?

Organize your thinking. What's your plan of action?

Proceed. Move forward, with increased clarity and under-standing.

Let's examine each step.

Step back

When you step back, you stop the momentum. You step out of the physical, mental, and emotional activity, the way a boxer in a ring steps back out of arm's reach for a second. When you step back, you are able to see things you couldn't see in the center of the fight. Now you have a different tactical perspective, and that gives you more options.

George, the CEO of a Fortune 500 company, came to our stress seminar and was initially put off by the STOP technique. He announced that it was nothing more than procrastinating, and he was way too busy to procrastinate. I talked about the purpose of STOP as a way to maintain balance and perspective. I explained that a STOP could just be a matter of stepping back for a few seconds—or even choosing not to act. George agreed to try, and came back to the seminar the next week feeling very satisfied with himself. He had used the STOP technique and it had worked for him. George described how his secretary had buzzed him one morning to tell him that one of his senior people was on the line. He immediately started to feel stressed. He stopped for a second to figure out why he was feeling that way, and realized that this particular manager only called him when he had a problem, and George was going to get involved in dealing with it. He told his secretary to tell the manager he couldn't talk to him. She asked him when he'd be available, and he replied, "Not today." His secretary was surprised, but she said okay. When George hung up the phone, at first he felt a little guilty, but then he was filled with relief. In fact, he did a little victory dance around his office, realizing that he had preserved his morning to do what he needed to do. Later in the week, the manager called again, and this time George felt no anxiety or stress. He took the call and learned that the manager had worked out the problem on his own.

George used a tactical step back, to give himself a little room. A bigger, more strategic, step back might be to take time off from work to reevaluate your goals. But even the briefest pause can be used to keep you connected with your purpose, and thus change the inevitable course of the stress responses.

Exercise: Use the Creative Stall

Practice for one day: With any stressful communication, pause for two or three seconds before you respond. Just the briefest pause can allow your brain to switch out of reactive mode and into conscious mode. At the end of the day, reflect on the differences you noticed in your conversations.

Think

Stepping back gives you a chance to think. In the space of focused thinking, you might ask yourself, "What is it in this situation that is causing me to feel fear, frustration, or pain? Why am
I doing this? What am I trying to accomplish? What are my obstacles? What are my inner and outer resources? What are my
options?"

The brilliance of the human brain is that we can create a place
to go where we can work things through. I call it a "think space."
Some people use a particular chair where they can be quiet and reflect. Some go to Starbucks to get a cup of coffee. I know of some
people who like to imagine they are in a helicopter flying above
their situation, and looking down from a distant perspective. Once
you've removed yourself from the unconscious momentum, you
can use thought to bring your consciousness to the equation.

Jennifer, a woman in our seminar, related how stressful it was
to have the annual telephone conversation with her ex-husband
about taxes. Inevitably, the discussion heated up, and she wouldn't
know what to say. Shortly after she was introduced to the STOP
tool, she found herself in the middle of the dreaded phone conversation. Feeling her stress rising, she said, "I'm going to put you
on hold for a minute." She walked away from the phone and jotted
down exactly what she wanted to say. When she returned, she
stated her convictions strongly and clearly. Her ex-husband was a
bit taken aback. He tried to outmaneuver her, which was his typical way, but she remained clear about her points and ended the discussion feeling satisfied. This was a first for her, and she felt very
proud of herself.

Exercise: Go to Your Think Space

Find a physical place that is removed from a stressful situation, a spot which for you is conducive to reflection. This
could be an office, a living room, or a bedroom, but even a

bathroom will do! Reconsider a stressful situation you identified in a previous exercise. Here are some questions that can be helpful to focus your reflection. It is worthy of note that thinking is not just reasoning or logic, but includes other ways of knowing, such as feeling, intuiting, and seeing.

- What's the truth about what is happening here?
- What am I feeling about this situation?
- What are my priorities?
- Are my actions or thoughts aligned with my priorities?
- What are the obstacles to moving toward my desired outcome?
- What assumptions am I making?
- What other action options do I have?
- What resources can I access, inner and outer?
- How can I enjoy myself in this situation?

Asking even a few of these questions can be enough to switch you from automatic to conscious action.

Organize your thoughts

Thoughts don't usually occur in a logical, sequential fashion. They need to be organized before meaningful action can happen. Let's say you go for a routine checkup and your doctor finds a suspicious lump. He wants to schedule you for a biopsy right now. Panic sets in. You start to sweat, you feel helpless, and you are terrified of not doing exactly as he says. Instead of reacting in a blind panic, you STOP and decide you have the option of seeking a second opinion. The second opinion may confirm your doctor's. It may not. That's not the whole point. The STOP will allow you to go from panic to a sense of control. Armed with two opinions, you can think, organize your options, and make a wiser decision.

Exercise: Organize

Having spent some time answering questions in your think space, ask yourself how you would organize these thoughts to proceed into conscious action.

Proceed

Now you are ready to act (or not act) based on your conscious choice. Even if at a later time you consider that you could have made a better choice than you did, you can still progress and learn something about yourself, and gain wisdom for the next time.

Once you have found clarity and are out of the stress reaction, take action. Reflection without action is like walking with one leg. Without action you don't accomplish and don't really learn. So, finish your conversation, go back to work, and continue with your day. The purpose of STOP is to be able to start again, with a clearer mind and a greater sense of purpose and control. Some managers I've coached at first worry that recommending the use of the STOP tool will give workers permission to slack off, or that they'll lose their edge. The opposite is true. When your environment is doing to you instead of you doing to your environment, mistakes get made. Mistakes eat up a lot of time. Taking a little time to be conscious saves much more time than it takes. Productivity increases when people are able to take a break, make a plan, and get control.

Exercise: Proceed

List one action you are prepared to proceed with in the immediate future. Be specific about each of the steps you will take to complete this action.

LONG STOPS AND SHORT STOPS

Some situations require a longer STOP—an hour, a day, a week, or even a month, depending on how significant the decision is. For example, if you are considering a major career change, a person close to you has become sick or has died, you are entering into a serious relationship or marriage, you are wondering about the purpose of your life, or if you find that your stress temperature is higher than is acceptable to you, you will need a longer STOP to get the clarity you need to choose the best action. In reading this book, you are already taking a STOP, which we hope will have a long-term beneficial effect.

Exercise: Choose Your STOPs

Sometimes STOP is like a shield that helps you escape from stress momentum. Other times we use it proactively to build stability and prevent stress from occurring. Using any of the tools recommended in this book requires first that you step back and reflect. Think about three times in your day when STOP would be useful, and plan ahead. For example:

- STOP at the beginning and end of each day to reflect and plan.
- STOP whenever you sense that you are caught in unconscious momentum and feel out of control.
- STOP before you go into a meeting, to think about the purpose, goals, and anticipated roadblocks.
- STOP before you pick up your child at school, to think about how you can create a meaningful moment with him or her before you both continue your day.
- STOP before you meet a friend for dinner, to think about the kind of conversation you want to have.

Once you get in the habit, you'll find yourself using STOP frequently, and you'll begin to notice a difference in the way you approach problems. One caution: Often when you most need to STOP, you are least likely to do it. In the heat of a stressful situation, with the Stress Maker carrying on, you might be tempted to charge ahead into the stress. But wise decisions and clear choices are missed often in this situation. The wisest action is to step back and reflect first. The outcome will always be better if you enter stress on your own terms.

ELEVEN

Inner Game Tool #2:
Being the CEO

You'll remember earlier we talked about what it would mean to be the CEO of your life—to say, in effect, "I'm in charge here." When we do this exercise in our stress workshops, the response is pretty amazing. People really get into it. Some actually set up a boardroom. One of my favorite stories came from a middle-aged businessman in one of our seminars, who was a manager at a large corporation. He described setting aside an hour to meet with his "vice presidents," and he went through the process. At our next session, he shared his discoveries with the group.

"One thing I saw was that I was letting my corporation be too much of a democracy," he said. "I was listening to everything that was said, giving it equal weight. I kept saying, 'Well, that sounds good, that sounds good.' I realized I was doing it, so I started taking more control, saying, 'No, this is the way it's going to be.' But it was very difficult, and after about a half an hour I started getting sleepy. That's when the Vice President of Criticism jumped in and said, 'You're supposed to be the CEO, but you can't handle this. You're buckling, you're crumbling.'

"I said, 'Shut up. I'm taking a nap.' I took a fifteen-minute nap and came back refreshed. Then I concluded business and wrapped up the meeting. That was interesting to me. I saw that I could take a break in the middle of a board meeting."

I got a kick out of this story. One thing I've learned from doing this exercise with groups is that people come away feeling good. They enjoy the control. It's not a headache.

Exercise: Using the CEO Tool

In this exercise I'm going to ask you to imagine yourself as the CEO of your life. Remember, you are the sole decision maker about the mission, products/services, policies, values, and priorities of your corporation. The first step is to call a meeting of your board of directors and staff, where *you* will set the agenda. Don't cede the CEO chair to the Vice President of Popularity, or the Vice President of Health, or the Vice President of Success. You can listen to their input, but you're in the CEO chair.

1. What is your mission statement?

Who are you? What is your primary mission in life? Another way of asking this is, what would make your corporation successful?

2. What is your primary product/service?

What does your personal corporation do? What is your vocation? This may change as the years go by, but the point is that you get to decide. So, start by evaluating what your corporation's primary task is now.

3. What are your policies and values?

Again, *you* get to decide. As CEO, you are in a position to review the values and policies that you've been using and make any changes you want. Is that too much power to assume? No. You are the one who adopted your values, consciously or not, and you have always been the one responsible for them.

Now, some of your vice presidents may not approve. One might say, "You act like you can decide the difference between right and wrong—isn't that God's job?" Ah, but which God are you choosing, which philosophy, which set of principles, which political party, which beliefs and ideals? It may sound like a bit of work, but that's what you'd do if you were the CEO of a company, and don't you think your life is at least as important as a company? You may have accepted some of these values very early on in life and never consciously reviewed them.

4. What are your priorities?

Which of the goals of your corporation are most important to you? Where do you want to focus your effort? It's all too easy to get fixated on what you think is the priority of the moment and forget about basic human needs, especially the need for self-actualization. Yet without paying attention to this need, meeting other priorities can feel meaningless.

5. What are your corporation's inner and outer resources?

Every corporation has resources. Look at the list of inner resources you developed earlier. These are available to you. How much are you drawing upon these resources? Which have you ignored? How might you use them to your benefit? What are the external resources you trust? Are you getting the benefit you could from them?

6. Who owns your corporation's shares?

Make a list of the shareholders of your corporation—the people who have an ownership stake in your life, who have votes in your decision-making process. Place a value on their ownership. Are most of the shares owned by your spouse, your parents, your boss, your children? Maybe the owners of your corporation are not people, but activities, concepts, or even addictions.

7. What did you sell your shares for?

What exchanges did you make? Did you sell shares for approval, for money, for love, for pleasure? Or did you sell shares to alcohol or other substances in exchange for a sense of comfort? This, too, is a matter of choice. For example, you may have said to your Vice President of Human Relations, "I need love in my life," and the vice president said, "Okay, to get love you have to do everything Tom says and be exactly the way Tom wants you to be. Then you'll get love." And maybe you'll say to the vice president, "Let's look at other options."

8. How can you buy shares back?

Choose an area where you think you've sold too many shares, and list the steps you will take to buy them back. For example, if you think you've ceded too much ground in a friendship in exchange for approval, you may have to trade some of the anticipated approval to get shares back. To buy back your shares, you have to be willing to pay a price. If you sold shares to someone so she would like you, you can announce, "I'm taking my shares back, like me or not." It doesn't mean you will be disliked, only that you're open to the possibility of being disliked in order to have those shares back. It is not always necessary to announce to the shareholders that you are buying back shares. Often they won't even be aware that they

% SOLD	TO WHOM ?	FOR WHAT?	BUY BACK (√)	ACTION

own them. A declaration to yourself is good enough to make the behavioral changes.

Like any CEO, you would be wise to have meetings from time to time. A meeting is nothing more than you sitting in the CEO chair and remembering that you are the boss of your life.

PATIENT FILE

from John Horton, M.D.

TAKING BACK HER LIFE

My patient Melanie was sick at least 20 percent of the time. When she had a cold, instead of getting over it in a week, it lasted three weeks. When she had an allergic reaction, it lasted two or three weeks. When she injured herself, she was slow to heal. It was very frustrating to Melanie, who was quite health conscious. She ate well and exercised regularly. She just couldn't understand why she had so many health problems.

I invited Melanie to attend our stress seminar, thinking it would help her. A few months later, I ran into her at a local coffee shop where she was with a group of friends. She called me over to the table and announced, "Dr. Horton, your stress seminar saved my life."

I was pleased but somewhat perplexed by the fervor of her endorsement. "What do you mean?" I asked.

Melanie replied in a very loud voice, "Thanks to you, I'm getting divorced!"

I laughed nervously. "Please don't say that so loudly. I want other people to take the stress seminar."

But Melanie went on to explain that the seminar opened her eyes. She realized that she had been expending all of her energy trying to get along with a man who didn't respect or listen to her. His attitude was, "My way or the highway."

After she made the decision to get a divorce, Melanie rarely came to our practice. As she took charge of her life, her medical problems began to ease. Her husband wasn't so happy with the situation. He visited me and said, "Dr. Horton, please have a talk with my wife and straighten her out. She has a crazy idea that she'll be better off on her own than living under my roof and doing things my way." For Melanie, it wasn't such a crazy idea. She had taken back ownership of her life.

The point of the CEO Tool is to help you become free and responsible in your life. It's often not easy to admit to yourself where and how you have eroded your personal freedom and responsibility, but the payoffs of doing so are enormous. It's difficult to be in a healthy relationship or to be part of an effective team if you aren't first secure in your independence as an individual. The importance of achieving this step cannot be over-emphasized. Independence is your primary defense against the powers of the Stress Maker, and is critical to your physical health and mental stability.

TWELVE

Inner Game Tool #3:
The Three Control Questions

RECENTLY, WE WERE CONDUCTING A STRESS SEMINAR, AND AFTER THE break one guy was missing. "Where's Joe?" I asked. A woman in the group went to find him and came back and said, "Joe says he's stuck on the phone." We had spent the whole morning talking about how to be the CEO of one's life, and there he was "stuck" on the phone. Since feeling stuck is one of the most stressful conditions, and he had agreed to be back from breaks on time, I gently suggested that he find a way to remove the glue that was sticking him.

How many times do you feel stuck? Stuck in a job, stuck in a relationship, stuck with obligations, stuck with a lousy hand of cards, stuck in your life? And how much stress is caused by not figuring out where you have control and where you don't?

As you go about your day, there are hundreds of things that are outside your control, but which are capable of causing stress:

- You don't control the traffic jams, which make you late for work.

- You don't control your boss's mood, which can upset your day.
- You don't control the health of the economy, which has serious implications for your financial well-being.
- You don't control the weather, which can spoil your weekend plans.

Many of the things we try to control have to do with the way we relate to others. For example, if you have a teenager, you realize that there are big control issues. That's natural. Teenagers are trying to grow up and assert themselves. Adults are trying to make sure they get there in one piece. Different agendas. Often, the more control parents try to assert, the more resistant teenagers become. Well, you might be thinking, "I control the car keys." True enough. Here's some of what you don't control:

- Your child's attitude
- Your child's motivation
- Your child's likes and dislikes
- Your child's respect for your opinions
- Your child's receptivity to listening

It's amazing when you consider how much energy goes into trying to control what we can't control. We say, "Why can't this person just act the way I want her to?" and we beat our heads against the wall, agitating about that. Or we're the guy in the traffic jam who keeps honking his horn, even though that doesn't make the traffic move.

THE CONTROL QUESTIONS TOOL

A simple tool for unburdening yourself from the stress of not being in control in any given situation is to ask three questions in the following sequence:

1. What *don't* I control here?
2. What am I currently *trying* to control?
3. What *could* I control that I'm not presently controlling?

Let me elaborate with an example.

A friend of mine is a stockbroker who lost a large amount of money in the 2008 market plunge. He not only lost money but also a great deal of confidence in his ability to trade successfully. He told me that he sometimes sat paralyzed in front of his computer screen for hours, wasn't sleeping well, and was imagining the worst of all possible outcomes. His mind was racing and obsessed with checking moment by moment the movements of the market. He felt compelled to try and earn back some of what he had lost. To say the least, his stress level was quite high. I asked him if he wanted to try using the control questions, and he agreed. Here are his results:

What don't I control?

- I don't control the swings of the market.
- I don't control the global economic ramifications of this recession.
- I don't control the money I have already lost.
- I don't control what my clients think about my capabilities.
- I don't control the inner voices telling me I'm a failure.
- I don't control how I feel about this situation.

What am I trying to control?

- I'm trying to control my thinking about when I should buy and sell.
- I'm trying to control my thoughts about a catastrophic future.
- I'm trying to control my ability to offer reassurance to my clients.

What could I control that I'm not controlling?

- I could accept the situation for what it is.
- I could take breaks away from the computer.
- I could take a weekend off and come back to the market with a fresh attitude.

- I could use medication to help me sleep and lower my anxiety.
- I could try to keep a separation between me, my self-esteem, and the market.
- I could stop listening to my own negative thinking.
- I could set realistic goals for trading in this volatile market.
- I could stop crying over spilt milk.
- Once relaxed, I could use my creativity to think of options.

He was pleased to discover that he could control so much that would improve his state of mind—which, he realized, was as much a torment for him as the market decline. Acting on what he *did* control restored a sense of confidence from which he could make the best of a bad situation.

It is not unusual at the end of answering the first two questions to feel small and helpless—at least humble—in the face of a difficult reality. But if you do a good job on the first two, the last question offers a chance for reflection time that often unlocks possibilities not before recognized—enough to set you on your way back to a realistic sense of control. Usually people find that the things they can't control lie outside them, and the things they haven't been controlling, but could, are within themselves. And the outcome will always be better when you enter stressful situations on your own terms.

Exercise: Using the Control Questions

Choose any situation that you find is considerably stressful and examine it from the perspective of the three control questions. Enjoy the process. Remember, there's nothing wrong with letting humor be your companion. Being able to laugh can be the doorway to understanding and humility.

What don't I control in this situation?

Make a list of everything that comes to mind, including other people's attitudes and actions.

What am I currently trying to control?

Make a list of what you are currently attempting to control, even if the items are also on the list of what you don't control.

What could I control that I'm not presently controlling?

Make a list of what you might control that you haven't before considered. Often, these will show up in a flash of insight. Don't be surprised if they are internal variables that you haven't thought of controlling.

Use the control questions to gain clarity and options. When you place your focus on what you can control, rather than what you can't control, new avenues open. You may be surprised to find that you then start influencing factors that you thought were beyond your grasp.

In our stress seminars, we use a powerful quotation from Epictetus, who was born a slave in the year AD 55 and became one of Rome's most prominent philosophers. The quotation is from the first chapter of a recent version of Epictetus's book, *The Art of Living*, and is a wonderful example not only of the issue of control in our lives but also how simple wisdom lasts through the ages. Epictetus might have been referring to the Inner Game when he wrote:

> *"Happiness and freedom begin with a clear understanding of one principle: Some things are within our control, and some things are not. It is only after you have faced up to this fundamental rule and learned to distinguish between what you can and can't control that inner tranquility and outer effectiveness become possible.*
>
> *"Within our control are our own opinions, aspirations, desires, and the things that repel us. These areas are quite rightly our concern, because they are directly subject to our influence. We always have a choice about the contents and character of our inner lives.*

"Outside our control, however, are such things as what kind of body we have, whether we're born into wealth or strike it rich, how we are regarded by others, and our status in society. We must remember that those things are externals and are therefore not our concern. Trying to control or to change what we can't only results in torment."

THIRTEEN

Inner Game Tool #4:
Trying On a New Attitude

EVERYBODY'S GOT ATTITUDES. IT'S A CONSTANT. AN ATTITUDE CON-sists of a set of fixed thoughts and concepts that influence our perceptions, emotions, reactions, and behaviors.

We have attitudes about what we do: Are we good enough to do it? Do we want to do it? Is it a hassle to do it? We have attitudes about the things that happen to us and how life treats us. In fact, when we wake up in the morning, we're already wearing an attitude. Maybe it's that everything is going to be wonderful that day. Or maybe it's that everything is going to be lousy that day.

We also have attitudes about ourselves—not just what we do or what happens to us, but who we are.

Attitude affects everything we do in the course of a day, and a lot of people think their attitude just is, for good or ill. It's part of who they are. But if you recognize that you are the CEO of your own life, you're free to consider where you came by an attitude and make any change you choose.

Let's say you're beset by stress, and you're wildly trying to manage your thoughts and feelings. Consider the analogy of an airplane flying in turbulence. The overhead compartments are popping open, and bags (thoughts and feelings) are randomly spilling out all over the place. You keep trying to put them back into the compartments, but as soon as you do, more spill out. You can't manage the chaos because the *attitude* of the plane is off—the nose is pointing too far down or up. To regain control of the plane's attitude, you have to become aware of the orientation of the plane as it is and then find the attitude lever.

What if you find your attitude and you don't like it? It's good enough to find it, good enough to become aware of it. Once you achieve awareness, change is not difficult.

In our stress seminar, we do an exercise called "trying on a new attitude." The instructions are simple. One person tells about a stressful situation and makes a best guess at what the overriding attitude is. Then the other participants suggest alternative attitudes that might fit the situation. The first person listens nonjudgmentally, "tries on" each attitude, senses how it feels to wear it, and then makes a selection that feels good to him or her.

In one seminar, we did the exercise with Fred, an editor in the magazine industry. Fred was very competent, but he found himself in a lull without a job. He contacted all the people he knew, but none of them had any work. He began to experience fear about finances, and even imagined the possibility of homelessness. He had been through this many times before, and something had always appeared, but he was getting older and his confidence was clearly shaken. I asked him about his attitude, and he replied, "My attitude is that this dangerous and scary thing has me in its grip."

So I then asked the others in the room to suggest fresh attitudes, and Fred, as if he were buying a suit, would try on each new attitude, and see how it felt and how it fit. The aim wasn't to find the right attitude, just one that felt good.

One person suggested, "The universe is protecting me," an attitude of complete trust that everything would be fine. Fred couldn't relate to it. He responded, "I'm in the wrong store!" But then other participants made suggestions that Fred could relate to:

"This is an opportunity to create a new source of income."

"I need to step out of the box to find a solution."

"I could turn to the creative genius that I usually save for magazine editing to solve this challenge."

Soon Fred had a fresh attitude that felt good for him to wear: "This is an opportunity to create a new income stream, and I will step out of the box and use my creativity to find it." He felt a lot more hopeful, and thanked the group for its help. The next time I saw him, he casually mentioned, "Oh, by the way, I have a new job."

Sherry, a woman in the same seminar, shared the struggle she had with her son. "One of his problems is a hormonal imbalance, which gives him a big tummy," she said. "His posture is bad, and this increases his problems." Sherry admitted that she often felt angry. She felt she knew what was best for her son, and he just wasn't cooperating. We talked about several attitudes Sherry might try on:

She could feel sorry for her son. Nope, she didn't like that one.

She could try to educate him. No, she'd already tried that and it didn't work.

She could be humble. He wasn't the kid she ordered, but he was a special human being. She liked that one.

She could use a different set of eyes to view her son—not looking at the outside, but looking at his inner qualities. She liked that one, too.

Sherry admitted that her attention had been so directed to her son's body that she hadn't been able to appreciate him as a person.

A NEW ATTITUDE IS ALWAYS POSSIBLE

Edd related a very touching and instructive story involving his then ten-year-old grandson, Austin. One day, Austin arrived home from a Boy Scout meeting in great despair. "I have no friends. I will never have friends," he lamented. Edd tried to find out what had happened. Austin said that his best friend was talking behind his back, and everyone was making fun of him. "Nobody likes me," he cried. Edd tried to help his grandson see the situation differently, but he just got angrier and more unhappy.

Then Edd asked, "Do you know the poem 'If' by Rudyard Kipling?" Austin hadn't heard of it, so Edd suggested he look it up on the Internet. Finally, that produced a smile. "Okay, if you promise not to tell Mom," he said. He wasn't supposed to have access to the Internet at that time of day, but Edd felt the lesson warranted breaking the rules.

Austin found the poem, and they read it together, line by line:

> "If you can keep your head when all about you / Are losing theirs and blaming it on you; If you can trust yourself when all men doubt you, / But make allowance for their doubting too; . . . Or, being lied about, don't deal in lies, Or, being hated, don't give way to hating . . ."

Edd could feel his grandson's energy completely changing as they read the poem. By the time they reached the final lines— "Yours is the Earth and everything that's in it, / And—which is more— you'll be a Man my son!"—he was back to his old self.

Austin printed the poem and said, "I want to be able to see this whenever I need to." He considered putting it on the ceiling above his bed, but the print was too small. Instead he tacked it on the wall right next to his bed, and went about enjoying the rest of his day.

Edd's experience with his grandson demonstrates how simple and natural it can be to shift from an attitude of despair to one of acceptance and challenge.

Exercise: The "Trying On a Fresh Attitude" Tool

Pick a circumstance or situation in your life that generates a lot of stress and tends to shake your inner stability. It might involve another person, a job, an activity you dread. It can be big or small. Define the stress.

Reflect honestly about your current attitude. You may have to dig for this, but you'll know when you find it. It will click for you. Make a note of it.

Now, go to your inner resources. Practice thinking of and trying on different attitudes. For example, if your typical attitude is resentment, what would it look like if you put on an attitude of gratitude before you went into the situation? Keep trying on attitudes until you find one that fits and feels good to you. Remember that feelings of fear, frustration, and pain trigger the stress system. If you wear an attitude that feels good to you, it will shield you from the stress system and its limited reactions of fight, flight, or freeze.

PATIENT FILE

from Edd Hanzelik, M.D.

A NEW ATTITUDE

Paul experienced two episodes of such severe chest pain that both incidents sent him to the hospital. He was afraid that something was seriously wrong, but the tests came back clean. It was conclusive that the pain was not coming from his heart.

I asked Paul, "What do you understand about this pain?"

He replied, "It is not physical."

"Well, from your description, I can tell that it *is* physical," I replied. "Maybe it is not your heart, but it's real pain in your body." Many patients have difficulty with the idea that stress has a physical impact—it's not "all in the mind."

I asked Paul about his level of stress. He began by saying he hated his job. He was a drama teacher, a hands-on person, passionate about his work. But due to financial cuts in the school system, he was not teaching drama. He was teaching keyboard and drafting in a room with no drafting equipment, and supervising a lunch period and two study hall periods. Everything he was doing was uninteresting and painfully boring to him. "I have no control," he said. "I don't control the principal, the rules, the finances. I don't control almost all of it."

I asked him, "What could you control that you are not now controlling?" His first thought, although he wanted to discount it, was his attitude. I spent time with that and took him through the attitude exercise. I tossed out possible attitudes for him to try on. The one that felt good to him was "This is happening for a reason, and I can benefit from it." At first he could not imagine benefiting from the work situation, but he opened up, tried on the attitude, and decided it felt okay.

"What about the pain? Can you have a new attitude toward the pain?" I asked. He didn't see how, but then thought it could be reminding him of something. I suggested perhaps it was a barometer of his stress. He liked that.

So Paul left with a lot to consider and some new tools, including trying on fresh attitudes. I encouraged him to get a fresh attitude in place before the onset of the next school year in three weeks. He was relieved to realize he was not helpless, that he could do something about his stress. Over the course of that school year, Paul was able to significantly reduce the stress he was experiencing. He shifted his attitude and focused on what was in his control. He found aspects of the work that were enjoyable and began to appreciate the decreased demands on him.

This is a common type of stress in which we find ourselves stuck doing something we don't want to be doing. We often don't see that the Stress Maker worsens the situation. Often, a simple shift in attitude can provide some relief. For Paul, a situation that had been intolerable, and which was contributing to his intense chest pain, was transformed into something bearable and even beneficial. Although his problem didn't disappear overnight, he felt confident that in time he could resolve it.

When people find an attitude that feels comfortable, they are surprised at how easy it is to wear it. They may default to their old attitude, but as soon as they notice it, they can shift back to their fresh outlook. This is an important component of a personal shield, helping to identify a source of stress and creating a protection against it. For me the attitude tool is extremely powerful. It helps me remember that I am in control of my attitude, which affects so much in my world. Being able to see one's attitude is the first and most important step. Once the attitude and the need for a change are seen, the change itself is relatively easy. Sometimes it's enough for me to just notice if my plane's orientation is up, down, or level. The needed adjustment is almost automatic.

FOURTEEN

Inner Game Tool #5:
The Magic Pen

THE MAGIC PEN TOOL IS ONE I USE AT THE BEGINNING OF ALMOST every day and at any other time when I need to access wisdom. It's a very simple exercise, done with pen and paper in a quiet place. I often call this "Self 2 writing."

Exercise: Using the Magic Pen Tool

1. Pick any difficult circumstance. It can be a person or a setting, something big or small—anything that needs a little wisdom instead of the usual commentary from Self 1. For example, your fifth grader brings home a D on his math test.

2. Take a minute to write down the normal conversation you might have about this situation—the running inner dialogue. Do this until the Self 1 concepts and ideas are at an end. It might go: *I knew this kid wasn't doing his homework when he said he was. I need to really apply some discipline here or he won't amount to anything. He's been getting his own way far*

*too much around here. I need to show him who's boss. If I let him
get away with this, it will set a precedent . . .*

3. When the Self 1 thoughts have run their course, stop and
imagine that you can endow your pen with selected inner
abilities. *Your* inner abilities. I often pick clarity, compassion,
and candor, but any qualities from your list of inner resources
will do. Imagine dipping your pen into each of your selected
resources. With an empty mind, allow your pen to write you
a message. Don't think about it. Just let it go. If you find
yourself with nothing to write, just keep writing. Let the
inner resources in the pen do the writing. Don't censor what
the Magic Pen writes. For example, if you endow your Magic
Pen with serenity, patience, and empathy, you might write
something like: *I know it's hard to be a kid. There are so many
distractions, so many things that seem more fun than studying. He's
not bad for wanting to watch TV instead of studying. I can help create an environment where it's easier for him to concentrate when he
has to and have fun when it's time for fun. No power struggles . . .*

The Magic Pen tool is a very practical way to learn how to tap
into your inner resources. It can help you distinguish for yourself
the difference between the tone and content of your Self 1 voices
and those of Self 2. When you compare the two writings, you
might find that you like some things written from Self 1, and don't
like some things written from Self 2. No problem. Both writings
were done without censorship. Just circle the parts of each that
feel good to you and make sense. Obviously, this is more an art
learned from experience than magic.

I once asked a large international audience of accountants to do
the Magic Pen exercise, and I invited people to share their Self 2
writing. The first person to get up, an East European, started with
an apology that he had been unable to write prose. What followed
were words that had the beauty and cadence of an artful poem that
moved much of the financial audience to tears. Self 2 can be full of
surprises when it isn't filtered!

PATIENT FILE

from John Horton, M.D.

A HEALING PERSPECTIVE

Some time ago, I saw Joan, a young woman in her early thirties who had a lump in her neck. It turned out to be Hodgkin's disease, which can be treated and cured. Joan had the lump removed, followed by a long course of chemotherapy, and she started to see me regularly. I didn't consider my role as a doctor managing a patient's illness. Rather, I viewed myself as a coach.

When her illness was diagnosed, Joan was in a complete state of exhaustion. Her answer was always yes whenever anyone at work asked for something. But now she began to see this as a time for taking care of herself, not other people, and with this understanding, a phenomenal change began to occur. When I invited her to do Self 2 writing, using the Magic Pen, here is what she wrote: "This is not something you have to be afraid of. It is what it is. It's natural to feel fear and even anger that this disease is keeping you from doing what you normally do. But these emotions are not *you*. They are just emotions that show how much you care about your life. You now have some time for yourself, to take care of yourself in a way you never allow yourself to. You can even have fun and let your husband and family help you. They'll feel good about it. This disease will pass, and you can take good advantage of your downtime."

There is no doubt in my mind that Joan's healing attitude contributed directly to her speedy recovery. There is much medical research to show that attitude is key to dealing successfully with a serious illness.

FIFTEEN

Inner Game Tool #6: Transpose

WITH ANY KIND OF STRESSOR INVOLVING OTHER PEOPLE—AND LET'S face it, there are very few that don't—it's effective to look at the situation through the eyes of the other person. Everyone perceives reality through their own grids, which involve thoughts, feelings, and intentions. But as human beings, we realize that others have different points of view than ours, and we can try to understand them. The ability to see a situation through another's eyes—empathy—is one of the most powerful qualities of being human. Besides feeling very good, empathy also gives you a greater range of choices about how you communicate with other people.

THE TRANSPOSE TOOL

The Transpose tool involves answering three questions from the perspective of the other person. These questions address three fundamental perspectives of being human—thinking, feeling, and intention. Using the first person, put yourself in the other's place and ask:

- What am I thinking?
- What am I feeling?
- What am I wanting?

Asking these questions allows you to see a situation through another's eyes and to access your empathy. It also gives you a greater range of choices about how you communicate with that person. Even if you don't agree with the other person, it is a relief to be clear about where he or she is coming from. It's similar to the Native American saying, "Never judge a man until you have walked a mile in his moccasins."

I recall a conversation with Derek, the sales manager for a software company. He was extremely frustrated by his boss's management style, which was very aggressive and critical. I asked Derek why he thought his boss behaved that way. He shrugged. "He's just a lousy manager," he replied. This assessment of his boss, accurate or not, didn't help Derek perform better or give him any clues about how to resolve his own stress. So I asked Derek to put himself in his boss's shoes for a moment. "You're the boss, sitting at your desk, and you ask your sales manager, Derek, to come in for a meeting. What are you thinking?"

Derek considered this for a minute, and then said, "I'm thinking that sales are down 20 percent over last year, and we have to try to get them back up."

"Okay," I said. "What are you feeling?"

"I'm feeling tense and worried about keeping my job!"

"So, what are you wanting from this meeting with Derek?"

"I guess I'm wanting Derek to help get me out of this mess," he replied thoughtfully. "I can't do it alone."

Performing this exercise had a profound effect on Derek. He began to see his own role differently—not just as the object of his boss's ire and a victim of his situation, but as a person his boss needed for his own and the company's success.

Transposing is a particularly useful tool for primary and family relationships. These are relationships where the most love is exchanged, but also where the most antagonism and stress can occur. To use the tool effectively, there can be no manipulative motives behind your effort—just the sincere desire to understand the other person.

A long time ago, my sister and her sixteen-year-old daughter were having a conflict about summertime curfew. My niece was dating, and she wanted to be able to stay out until 11:00 p.m. Her mother wanted her home before 10:00 p.m. My sister asked me for advice about how to resolve this ongoing conflict. "I just don't feel I'd be doing my duty as a mother to give in on this one," she told me. "And I know how easy it is to get carried away on a summer's night. Most of all, I don't like the ongoing conflict with my daughter." I asked her to Transpose her daughter. It came out something like this:

"I am thinking that my mother doesn't trust me to control the situation with my date. I am thinking I should keep pressing her until she does.

"I am feeling hurt and rebellious. I'm feeling I can trust myself.

"I am wanting to prove to myself and my mother that I can be trusted to stay out until 11:00 p.m. without getting into any trouble."

When I spoke with my niece, I discovered that my sister's transposing of her was pretty accurate. I then asked her to Transpose her mother. Here's what she said:

"I'm thinking that it's my duty as a mother to keep an early curfew.

"I'm thinking that I didn't get to stay out so late when I was her age.

"I'm thinking that I couldn't always stay out of trouble at that age.

"I'm feeling that I love my daughter and care about what happens to her.

"I'm feeling afraid that she may be overconfident about herself and might get into trouble.

"I'm wanting to be a good mother and protect my daughter."

So, what were the results? In the end, both held their ground. The curfew wasn't changed, and my niece kept asking from time to time. But there was a huge difference in the kind of conversation they had. It was no longer a fight, but a discussion between two strong women who truly respected each other's point of view. The struggle was over.

Transposing yourself

It is also possible to Transpose yourself, to get a clearer picture of what you are really thinking, feeling, and wanting in any situation. To do this, you step outside yourself, as if you are looking down from above to get the widest possible perspective, and ask in the third person:

- What is *he/she* thinking?
- What is *he/she* feeling?
- What is *he/she* wanting?

We hardly ever get enough distance from ourselves to be truly objective. This tool can help.

Exercise: Transpose and Transform

List three people you could Transpose on a regular basis to help your ongoing relationship. Pick one of them who is evoking some stress to Transpose now.

Put yourself in the other person's shoes and ask the three transposing questions: What am I thinking? What am I feeling? What am I wanting?

Did you gain any new insight about this person or about your choices in how to communicate effectively with him or her? If not, try again and take another look. Remember that people can always change according to time and the specific circumstance as they see it.

Although transposing is a very simple exercise, it takes both humility and courage to do it well. One cause of stress is the assumption that we know another person, even though we haven't looked closely. The more we Transpose, the more natural it becomes.

SIXTEEN

Inner Game Tool #7:
Redefine

The Redefine tool is indispensable in the quest to build stability—to establish a firm ground to stand on, so that you will not topple when the wind comes. It is based on the fact that we all carry with us certain lenses or definitions through which we look at ourselves, other people, activities, and events of our lives. These definitions not only color the way we see things, they limit the possibilities of our responses. Our lenses can be conscious, but are more often unconscious. Stereotypes are a blatant example of preconceived definitions passed down from one generation to another until they automatically dominate the way we view the world. The purpose of the Redefine tool is to bring our key definitions into conscious awareness so that we can let go of what isn't aligned with our current commitments and to allow us to choose what is.

Here is a quaint example of unconscious definition that makes the process clear. Every Thanksgiving, a husband asked his wife why she cooked the turkey with the legs cut off the body. Why, he asked, couldn't she serve it like everyone else, as a whole turkey?

His wife always replied defensively, "That's the way my mother taught me it should be done." This didn't satisfy her husband. One year he decided to explore the question further. "Let's ask your mother," he suggested. They called her mother, who confirmed, "Yes, that is right, we always cut the turkey legs off before cooking." When asked why, she said it was the way her mother taught her, and her mother was an excellent cook. The husband, wanting to get to the bottom of the question once and for all, called his wife's eighty-three-year-old grandmother, who said, "Oh, yes, when I was young we always used to cut the legs off the turkey before putting it into the oven, because in those days, ovens just weren't large enough!"

You might be surprised to see how many processes, policies, and rules in your own life are predicated on conditions that no longer exist, but where the definition didn't change with the times.

THE REDEFINE TOOL

When you're using the Redefine tool to build stability, follow these steps:

1. Identify the current definition or concept (turkey legs should be cut off before putting the turkey in the oven).

2. Find out where that definition came from in the first place (in this case, grandmother).

Now, take it further.

3. Ask yourself, "Is this current definition in line with my present circumstances and commitments (I have a larger oven and want the turkey to look as good as possible)?"

4. If not, Redefine to bring your definition into alignment with your circumstances and commitments (the whole turkey is okay).

5. Apply the new definition to the way you look at reality.

The Redefine tool helps you reclaim ownership and responsibility for how you see and delineate things. It teaches you that your definitions make a big difference, and that you have a choice of which lens you use in any situation. Again, when in a stress reaction, we want to change or run away from something outside, or we are so shut down we don't know what to do. The Redefine tool helps you to shift attention to what you do have control over.

A woman in our seminar, during a process of Redefining selfishness, once blurted out, "By my old definition, it's selfish to breathe!" Everyone laughed, but there was an important insight there. If it is called "selfish" to breathe, then maybe sometimes being "selfish" is not always the wrong thing to do. Or put another way, doing what is necessary for our health and well-being is not really selfish as long as we don't harm another person's chances to do the same. Consider what your redefinition of "selfish" would be.

Exercise: Redefine a Stressful Concept

The purpose of this exercise is to take a word that is frightening, frustrating, or painful to you and continue to Redefine it, using inner resources, until it is no longer stressful.

A few brief examples from the stress seminar:

Word: Selfish

Usual Definition: Thinking only of yourself.

Redefinition: Taking care of your basic needs so you can give more.

Word: Guilty

Usual Definition: Committing a "crime" that you will always carry with you.

Redefinition: Making a mistake that you can learn from and rectify.

Word: Fear

Usual definition: A bad emotion indicating weakness and insecurity.

Redefinition: An inner barometer of safety, an indicator of a challenge at hand.

First, identify a few people or activities that may be provoking your stress. Choose a key word related to your stress that you can redefine. It could be "boss," "money," "spouse," "doctor," or whatever you select. Then follow the five steps.

1. Identify the current definition you are using.
2. Where did you get it?
3. Is it in line with your current commitments and priorities in life?
4. If not, Redefine.
5. Apply your redefinition to change your perception of the stressful relationship or situation.

PATIENT FILE

---

from Edd Hanzelik, M.D.

REDEFINING GREATNESS

Here is an example of how a patient was helped by Redefining what it meant to be a great mother. On her first visit, Sarah was distraught and tearful. She had written a long list of all of her symptoms, and did not understand why she felt so bad. As I took a comprehensive history to understand the factors affecting her, I discovered she had six children and wanted above all else to be a great mother. If she sat down even for a second, she felt guilty that she wasn't doing enough. Sarah seemed quite surprised when, in our initial meeting, I told her that I believed all the symptoms on her long list were due to stress and exhaustion, and that my prescription was for her to take much better care of herself.

In effect, I was asking Sarah to Redefine her idea of what it meant to be a great mother. Sarah's current definition was "being totally focused on the needs of my family." With some coaching, she realized that the best thing a mother could give her children was a genuinely healthy and happy mother. Her Redefinition was simple: "As a mother, I'm an important part of the family, and I need to be taken care of." She could see that such a mother would be emotionally lighter, easier to get along with, much more accepting, kinder, more playful and understanding. Her love would flow easily because she felt good herself. That's what the whole family needed.

Sarah realized the only way she was going to be happy and healthy was to recognize and respond to her own needs. She had to put herself much higher up on her list of priorities. Her husband became a great help, giving Sarah support and encouragement. They both understood that she could not take care of the family if she herself was running on empty. I was gratified to see the profound transformation in Sarah's physical and emotional health as she embraced her new definition of motherhood.

It is always possible to Redefine. And it is a wonderful experience, like breathing new air. I had a very dramatic experience with redefining when my children were teenagers. I had been on a work trip in Copenhagen, and was about to come back home to join my family for Christmas. But I noticed that I wasn't looking forward to seeing my son and daughter. In fact, I was feeling a little stressed and burdened about it. "Why?" I wondered. "How am I looking at my children that would make me feel this way?"

I took a moment to reflect. The thought that came to me was a bit confronting: "Your current definition of your children is 'problems to be solved.' " Wow! It rang true. When one of them would knock at my bedroom door, I'd instantly expect a problem. And that made my definition of father "problem solver."

I asked myself where I got that perspective, and I saw that I came by it honestly. My own father had a tendency to look at me in that way.

I asked myself if I could come up with a better definition. I finally came up with this idea: "My children are my only chance to experience the love that can take place between father and son, and between father and daughter. They're my only shot at parental love." That was a big surprise. This new definition didn't have anything to do with changing my description of my children—just the lens through which I had been looking at them without even knowing it. This new definition felt much better, and I could see it was more in line with my current commitment to enjoy my life and family to the maximum.

So I went home for Christmas that year with excitement and anticipation. And then—what surprised me—was that for some unexplained reason, when the knocks came at the door, problems did not walk in, but real people for whom I had real feelings.

SEVENTEEN

Inner Game Tool #8:
The PLE Triangle

THE IDEA OF THE PLE TRIANGLE CAME FROM A PENETRATING question about the Inner Game asked by an interested business-man. "So, what does the Inner Game actually do?" he asked, try-ing to boil it down to a simple statement. I didn't have a ready answer, and had to reflect on the question for a while. I thought back to people who had had breakthroughs using the Inner Game. Then I answered, "Three things actually happen at the same time when the Inner Game is being played well. Performance is excel-lent, learning is occurring naturally, and enjoyment is present."

It was as if Self 2 were answering the question for the first time. And as I thought about it more, I realized it formed a nice defini-tion for work, play, or any human activity. I saw how much I, too, had been influenced by the cultural notion that performance was the only thing that counted. Work equaled performance, and suc-cess was judged by performance-related results. But, in fact, while you are working, you are also either learning or not. Likewise, while working, you are having some kind of experience, somewhere between misery and fulfillment. When I looked at children, I saw that all three—performance, learning, and enjoyment—were inherently important to the developing child and tended to happen simultaneously.

It's no secret that learning and enjoyment get left out of most people's definition of work. Using the PLE triangle as a tool is a way to find balance in any activity—a balance that is simply more human than taking any one side of the triangle and putting all your eggs in that basket. Performance occurs in the outer world. The bridge gets built, the product sold, the food put on the table. There is no argument about the necessity of performance goals. But there's also plenty of justification for setting learning and enjoyment goals. These are experienced on the inside, but they are just as valid as external results.

Many people do not consider enjoyment a necessary part of performance. That's especially true in America, where we are influenced by the Puritan work ethic. The New England philosopher George Santayana once wrote this definition of a Puritan: a person who has a gnawing fear that somewhere, somehow, someone is enjoying himself.

The PLE triangle consists of three equally important elements:

Performance: The actual "doing" itself.

Learning: What you're learning or unlearning while doing.

Enjoyment: The quality of experience you are having while doing.

A single mother who attended our workshop told this story. One day she received a call at work that her son had been suspended from school for the day and she needed to pick him up right away. As she drove toward the school, she felt anxious and somewhat angry. But remembering the PLE tool from the workshop, she

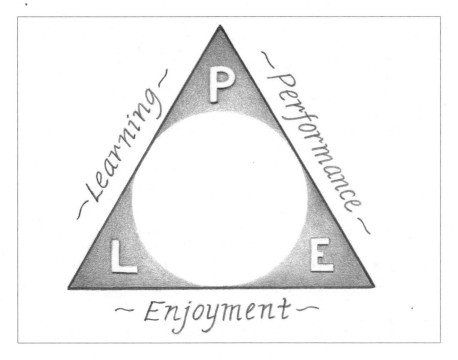

found herself thinking about how to use it so she wouldn't completely stress out.

Her immediate performance goal was simple. Her son had already been suspended for the day, and there was nothing she could do to change that. She realized, however, that she did have a learning goal. She had very little idea what life at school was like for her son. She'd been too busy to stop and listen. And she didn't know what had happened on that particular day to cause the suspension. She had a lot to learn and she was interested.

When she considered the enjoyment goal, she realized with a sense of pleasure that she and her son were free from work and school for the day, and had a rare opportunity to spend it together. They could have an adventure.

You can imagine her son's amazement when his mother arrived, smiling, and announced that they were going to lunch at his favorite restaurant. They ended up having a wonderful talk, and she learned many things about her son that day. She learned enough to have an informed conversation with her son's teacher about the particular episode that led to the suspension.

Exercise: Using the PLE Tool

Most of the time, our stress starts with an imbalance where the performance part of the triangle overwhelms everything else. That's our social conditioning. So, in this exercise, I want you to choose an area where you experience performance stress. It can be anything—a family struggle, a work project, even a weight-loss goal.

- What is your performance goal? Choose objectively, what you want to accomplish.
- What are your learning possibilities? You can choose what you want to learn from the experience that could be valuable to you.
- What are your enjoyment possibilities? What positive experience would you like to have in the process of performing and learning?

At first, just out of habit, your focus on performance might overwhelm learning and enjoyment. But if you make an appropriate commitment to all three, soon you will find a balance in which each side of the triangle is supported and even augmented by the other. After all, it is fun to perform well and to learn. And learning is bound to improve performance over time. All in all, you are taking more charge of your life. You become more of a human *being*, not just a human *doing*.

EIGHTEEN

Applying the Tools:
Eileen's Story

WHEN YOU HAVE A GOOD TOOLBOX, YOU CAN PULL OUT ANY TOOL AT the moment it's needed. I've found that usually STOP is the first one people use, because it provides space to consider the others. Then it becomes a creative exercise to discover which other tool is most effective in providing a shield or in building long-term stability.

I recently had the rare opportunity to sit down and interview one of John and Edd's patients and listen to her speak for herself about the way her application of the Inner Game tools improved her medical condition. Eileen impressed all of us when she attended our workshops: Here was a woman raised in extremely harsh circumstances, and whose family life in adulthood continued to be a trial. Her high levels of stress were manifested in severe medical conditions. Yet her commitment to being well—to living in Self 2—became an inspiration to everyone in the group.

An attractive fifty-five-year-old woman, Eileen first came to see Edd five years ago as an unscheduled emergency patient. He remembers her being doubled over in pain, weeping uncontrollably and groaning out loud. She had a complicated medical history, including several surgeries, gastric reflux, and chronic intestinal distress. This petite woman was on sixteen medications, and her other doctors had told her they couldn't help her anymore. After a thorough examination and many tests, Edd concluded that Eileen suffered from irritable bowel syndrome, a condition greatly exacerbated by stress. As he learned more about her, he found her story to be literally hair raising. It was no wonder that her stress levels were off the charts.

Today, Eileen is no longer the distraught, ill person who showed up at Edd's office. She no longer has abdominal pain or intestinal symptoms. Her energy is good and her spirits are very positive. She is a different person. How did Eileen overcome such tremendous physical problems? A major factor in Eileen's well-being has been her understanding of the role stress played in her sickness, and her commitment to using the Inner Game tools to support her recovery.

When I interviewed Eileen, I found an inspiring real-life example of someone who was actively engaged with the Inner Game. She was eager to share her story with others—to show them it was possible to make fundamental changes even after a lifetime of stress.

MY INTERVIEW WITH EILEEN

"Did you realize stress was a major factor in your illnesses?" I asked Eileen.

"No. I was in total denial," she replied. "I didn't know I was so stressed out. In fact, I thought I handled stress well. What a joke! I wasn't handling it at all, and it was taking me down."

"What was the biggest contributor to your stress?" I asked.

"I was under high tension for my whole life," Eileen said. "I was one of the older daughters out of twelve children in a dysfunctional family. Our father would get abusive and beat us. I took it on myself to be the protector and carried the world on my shoulders, even as a young girl. I couldn't say no. I had no boundaries. I felt so overwhelmed. I was so sick when I came to Dr. Hanzelik—and I was in despair because none of my other doctors could help me. I felt like a prisoner in my own world."

"How did you begin to get well?" I asked.

"When I first saw Dr. Hanzelik, he took time with me. I felt his listening validated me and I believed him when he told me I could get better. First, I had to accept that *I* existed. Before I started seeing Dr. Hanzelik, I wasn't even in the picture. I didn't have any control. And I had to accept that I needed help. I had done a lot of soul-searching in my life. I felt I was ready to learn. The entire team in Dr. Hanzelik's office helped me."

"When you were so sick, how did you find the energy to help yourself?" I asked.

"Just doing something helped me to feel some energy. The Stress Seminar gave me tools to help myself. The STOP tool was especially valuable in the beginning. I could step back and think clearly before I would say yes to another commitment. The Control Questions also helped me greatly. I kept reminding myself that I couldn't change others. They had to change themselves. That was a big one for me. I had been trying to fix my family for so long I didn't even know there was another way. More recently, I had been involved in helping my fourteen-year-old niece, who had a lot of problems. Not only was she not cooperating at times, but the other members of the family were angry with me and blamed me when things got worse. This was a major source of stress for me, and it helped to understand that I couldn't change them—only myself. So I started to take active steps to help myself. Among the steps I took were nutritional changes, attending health workshops, learning to meditate, seeing a psychologist, and visiting a spa. I began to see Dr. Horton for more stress counseling, and I attended his workshops for people with emotional wounds. I discovered I could stop being so reactive to everyone's needs.

"I immediately embraced the tools of the stress workshops. One of the first things I learned was the importance of awareness, choice, and trust. I have these beautiful little words in my mind for always now, which really helps me. I'm aware of what is happening around me, as well as to me. I'm much more aware of what is happening to my body. Before, I couldn't even feel my body until something happened that was so physically bad that I was on the ground. I couldn't even feel my own pain.

"Choice was a big one. Before, if someone called in a panic, I would jump into my car to rush to their aid, talking to them on my cell phone on the way to their house. Now I'm more apt to consider other options, such as saying, 'I can't come over right now, but I can pray with you on the phone.' I discovered that I couldn't be everyone's rescuer anymore.

"I learned that I needed a shield to protect myself. I was so afraid that wanting to take care of myself was very selfish. I remember crying because I thought I was being selfish. I even began to question my own existence. I wondered how I could feel like a loving person when I hadn't felt a lot of love in my own life. I examined every phase of my life and discovered I had a belief system that I had never questioned. I had voices all over my head, with everybody else's opinion telling me everything I should be doing and shouldn't be doing. You call it the Stress Maker. I started seriously questioning all my beliefs and found my own place in my own life. I learned to trust myself.

"The Attitude Exercise also helped me a lot. I made a sign and put copies around my house to remind myself to use the tools. At the center of the sign was the question, 'What attitude are you flying at?' Around the sides were Awareness, Choice, and Trust. People thought I was crazy, but I needed to do it. I even handed out signs to everyone in my stress seminar. I remember telling the class, 'These tools are working. I'm working with them and they are helping me.' I realized I had to do the exercises and the homework, and practice the tools. I couldn't go back. I didn't have a choice but to keep going forward," she said, becoming a little teary.

"I can see how the tools have helped you cope," I said. "But tell me, how did that translate into relief from your medical symptoms?"

"I always had tremendous pains in my shoulders and stomach," Eileen said. "When I first came to the doctors' practice, I couldn't stand up straight. My hair was falling out. People told me how ill I looked. I would get into the car and cry because of how bad I felt. I was so sick I couldn't eat anything. My stomach wouldn't handle food. It was like a fire burning. I came to see that stress really does have a physical manifestation. It was as if the worries in my mind made a beeline to my gut. Now I walk taller. I feel everything about me is lighter. I don't have any pain in my shoulders or stomach anymore. People tell me how good I look, and I feel good, too. I discovered my mind was the biggest problem. I didn't know that at all. Now I feel I have a healthier mind and body."

Sitting there, face to face with Eileen, I could see she was relating a true story—she really had taught herself to apply the Inner Game tools. But I pressed her. "I think some readers will look at your story and think it sounds too easy," I suggested. "What would you say to them?"

She laughed. "Oh, it hasn't been easy," she assured me. "I have had setbacks, just as any other person would. The biggest challenge came with a recent family crisis. At first I just couldn't handle it. I was so overwhelmed I couldn't use the tools. All of my stress symptoms came back—the shoulder and stomach pains, the anxiety, the digestive problems, and depression. I did not want to go back into stress, but I didn't know how to stop it.

"I picked up the phone and called Drs. Hanzelik and Horton. They counseled me on using the tools. I started to see a psychologist again, and I reentered the stress seminar, which was very helpful. I did the Attitude Exercise with the whole class helping me, and my attitude shifted. My fresh attitude was that I could handle this and that my family and I would learn and benefit from it. That felt good and I have stuck with it. Now I feel I have recovered my balance. Once you experience life without all the stress, you don't want to go back to the stress."

That statement impressed me. *Once you experience life without all the stress, you don't want to go back to the stress.* Exactly! It's a choice between being devastated by circumstances and finding control and even contentment in the midst of them. Eileen's brave efforts demonstrate how meaningful the Inner Game tools can be—and there is no question that her reliance on the tools made a real difference in her ability to overcome the substantial challenges that faced her. She had clearly become the CEO of her life and bought back shares from those she was trying so hard to please. She had redefined what it meant to her to really help someone else. Learning and enjoyment had taken their place alongside performance in all her activities. The Control Questions, the Attitude Exercise, and ACT had initiated a powerful learning process, in which she had taken advantage of many other resources. Her discovery of how to reduce her stress had a profound effect on her physical, mental, and social well-being and her enjoyment of life. Her enthusiasm was contagious—it made me happy to see someone taking full advantage of the toolbox.

How each person uses the tools is completely individual. There isn't a cookie-cutter formula for reducing stress. But we know that if you learn how to gain access to your inner resources and continually improve your stability, you will be able to go through challenges without being toppled. You will discover that you, too, have a choice when it comes to stress.

"My world changed," Eileen told me, with enthusiasm and sincerity. "I realized that my purpose isn't so much to assist everyone, but rather to be healthy enough to be able to help others in a conscious way. That's part of my personal shield—that I now know what I can do, what I can't do, and what I can receive. My being open to receiving is a big part of it. That was new for me. I've also been able to say no and walk away from some of the people who were not helping my life. That was a big step for me. Before I was living life from my gut, from my emotional reactions. I discovered I could live from my heart. That felt so much better."

Self 1 often uses one side of the PLE triangle to the exclusion of the others. The result can be an unsustainable imbalance in one's health and well-being. During one of our stress seminars, an executive reported that his successful career in real estate development became totally overwhelming and unprofitable when he let the ambitions of Self 1 consume him totally. He described how he seriously overextended himself on a project. Not only did he lose a lot of money, he collapsed into a depression due to his losses. Now back to living a balanced life, he summarized his experience with a warning to others: "Don't replace the E for Enjoyment in the PLE triangle with E for Ego."

Exercise: Applying the Tools

Pick the circumstance in your life that is causing you the greatest concern. Then pick two to three tools from the toolbox to apply in this situation.

Before you start, consider these two questions:

1. What is my level of confidence that applying the tools will help, on a scale of 1 to 10?
2. What is my degree of commitment to following through with applying the tools in my life, on a scale of 1 to 10?

NINETEEN

Applying the Tools:
Matters of Life and Death

W‏HEN‏ I ‏FIRST‏ ‏DEVELOPED‏ ‏THE‏ I‏NNER‏ G‏AME‏, I ‏REALIZED‏ ‏THAT‏ ‏ITS‏ application went beyond hitting balls. It was an approach that worked in all areas of life. The doctors, John and Edd, have enhanced my appreciation of that fact. They deal in life-and-death matters every day. It is at these moments that people often reflect seriously on the quality of their lives. In the game of life, the Inner Game tools are designed to facilitate, even in such moments, a response that has no regrets.

from John Horton, M.D.

ROBERT KNOWS BEST

Many years ago, I was asked by a colleague if I would take over the home care of Robert Young. Most people of a certain age will remember Young as the actor in the television series *Father Knows Best*, and later as the family doctor in the series *Marcus Welby, M.D.* Playing fictional characters, Robert Young had become a real-life icon nonetheless, representing the perfect father and the perfect doctor. Although I had years of experience as the codirector of a medical hospice, I felt a little bit intimidated. I'd often heard people compare doctors unfavorably to Marcus Welby.

Robert Young himself dismissed any claims to greatness. In fact, he said many times over the years that he was not the father he portrayed; nor did he have the wisdom of the doctor. He had had problems with alcoholism and depression, and had expressed his dismay in interviews that people could not separate the TV personality from the real less-than-perfect person.

When I first went to see him, Robert was quite aged. He was no longer drinking, and his depression was not an issue. He had a lovely home and some very devoted and capable caretakers. I found him kind, charming, and affable.

I took care of Robert for three years and developed a good rapport with the staff. Over time, we decided to allow him to be as he wished—not to push him to get up and exercise or do anything he didn't want to do. He really liked to rest in bed and slept a lot, peacefully, like a child. When he did get up, he would eat a hearty meal, watch television, and visit with friends. In the last months of his life, he didn't want to leave his bed, and we just took care of him there. One day when I came to visit, Robert woke up bright and cheerful. I asked him casually how he was feeling. He looked at me with a beautiful expression of contentment on his face and replied, "Perfect." Indeed, when he did finally die, it was without a sigh, a groan, or a ripple of pain. The staff was present, and it was so quiet and beautiful that we spontaneously applauded. Someone exclaimed, "Great exit, Robert!"

Our effort with Robert Young was to allow his last years to be as stress-free as possible. No one asked him to do things that frustrated his desire to rest and relax. It is known that when even the most stressed brain is allowed to unwind, much past suffering can be erased and new brain circuits encouraged to grow.

There is now a wonderful movement to create "social" hospice care, to give people who are dying the environment at home or in a hospice to let go of unfinished business and to evolve out of suffering, and the chance to leave their lives in a state of peace and love. I have seen this happen again and again when there is sufficient time and understanding to allow for this kind of departure.

On the other hand, when fear, frustration, and pain are driving the stress system at such a vulnerable time, then the derivatives of fight (anger, bitterness, complaining), or flight (overuse of drugs, wild imagination, dissociation), or freeze (anxiety, despair, depression) make the leaving process difficult for everyone. There are real choices about how we want to evolve even in the last months, weeks, days, and hours of our lives.

THE INNER GAME OF AGING

My early work with the Inner Game was mostly with younger people in a sports context, so the issue of getting older didn't come up. Later, when I began to coach in corporate settings, I noticed right away that older workers had a definite attitude about aging that was adding to their stress. It was "I am past my prime." I remember one guy, an extremely successful and capable manager, saying, "I turned fifty last week. It's all downhill from here." Now, objectively, he wasn't any different than he'd been a week earlier. In fact, my observation was that, at fifty, he was at the top of his game. But it didn't matter. He was sideswiped by a number. The difference was in his attitude.

The social pressure that comes with aging is real. But it's a stressor, separate from who we really are. When it comes to aging, we don't have to buy in to the voices of the Stress Maker. We can bypass them.

The way many people approach growing older reminds me of the performance pressure that interferes with playing tennis. They think too much about their movements, try too hard to control the game, worry too much about the results of their actions and their self-image. These are all doubt-driven interferences that undermine playing the game well.

TOOLS FOR AGING

It is possible to live your later years without that interference, as a pure Self 2 that isn't undermined by the voices of Self 1. Here the PLE triangle is a very useful tool. It may be true that you can't perform in some areas with the same skill as you grow older, but you can create new performance goals. And when you give equal weight to the other two components, enjoyment and learning, new opportunities open up to you. Enjoyment is possible until the day you die, as is learning. You can say, "I am not going to let stress rob me of the chance to enjoy this great gift of life."

The Attitude tool is also very helpful here. Try on a new attitude about aging. For example:

"I have more wisdom now, and I can share it with others."

"I have more time to reflect and discover my inner resources."

"I have a second chance to know what I knew as a child: Life itself is enjoyable for no particular reason—being here is the big deal, and I can move from one enjoyment to the next seamlessly."

"I can let go and resolve the pains of my life and find the peace I need to live and leave gracefully."

A ninety-year-old man once said to me, "I no longer care what people think of me. I can say anything I want." This happens a lot with very old people. They let go of all the fears and judgments and return to just being themselves.

PATIENT PROFILE

from John Horton, M.D.

CHANGING AN ATTITUDE TOWARD DEATH

Kathy was a forty-five-year-old woman diagnosed with multiple sclerosis who was waking up with panic attacks almost every night. She was very afraid after the diagnosis, even though a top specialist at UCLA had told her it was a rather mild presentation and she should have a normal life span.

When she awoke at night, Kathy was consumed by fear, not of disability, but of death itself. Instead of trying to convince her that she had no cause for fear, I discussed the Inner Game approach, and asked Kathy to try on new attitudes toward death and see if she could find one that she could wear as a shield at night.

I began to suggest some possible attitudes. "How about when you die, you go to heaven?"

"I don't believe that," she replied.

"How about when you die, you just go back to atoms and nothing else exists?"

"That's what I'm afraid of," she exclaimed. "It doesn't work."

Finally, I suggested this attitude: "That you have been alive for over forty years. Something kind has taken care of you, and perhaps when you leave, this same kindness will continue to take care of you."

Kathy smiled. "I like that," she said.

I told her that all the research on near-death experiences support that attitude. The consistent elements are that the peace and light people felt was very kind, and that the kindness was directed toward one's enjoyment of life and learning to love. She liked that, too.

The panic attacks ended as quickly as they began, as Kathy substituted a conscious attitude for the one she had been wearing unconsciously. I have known her for ten years, and she has had no more panic attacks since that day.

My experience with Kathy reminded me of a famous Chinese story, which tells of a loyal and wise minister being led to his execution by the guards of a foolish emperor. The wise minister stops to admire the plum blossoms, and a guard asks him, "Why are you admiring the plum blossoms when you are going to die?" He replies, "What else should I be doing?"

A FRESH DEFINITION

Jack, a corporate executive in his mid-forties, was obsessed with his age to a degree that seemed extreme. He was youthful, successful, and in apparently good health, and there seemed no obvious reason for him to be so worried. I wondered what definition Jack was employing that contributed to his stress. With some exploration, Jack revealed that his father had died of a heart attack at age fifty-two, and since that time, Jack had viewed his own life as being on a short leash. Even though he was very fit, and his doctors assured him that he was in good health, he couldn't shake the idea that a hereditary monster would take him, too. I asked Jack to consider a new definition that would be consistent with his circumstances and commitments—a definition that would be his alone, not his father's. The exercise astounded him, and was very freeing. He had never thought about his own prospects apart from what had happened to his father. He decided he was living a healthy life, and beyond that his time of death was not in his control.

A friend who was approaching sixty-five was growing depressed because in his business that meant forced retirement. For many people, the idea of retirement is damaging to the self. The word itself is negative. It means, literally, lying down, ceasing to produce and achieve. Being put out to pasture. No wonder older people feel ashamed. It is especially insulting today, when people can live vigorously well into their eighties and beyond. Employing the Redefine tool, I asked him if there was another definition he could give to retirement, and he came up with the idea that retirement meant a "second life." This definition granted him the mobility to approach his coming years with enthusiasm and optimism.

YOU'RE STILL IN CHARGE

When you're the CEO of your life, you run the show, whether you're twenty, forty, sixty, or beyond ninety. You can't be fired or dismissed from your own life. You're sitting at the head of the table until you die. The people around you may have opinions, but you get to decide the mission and activities of your life.

A friend of mine, a former company president who was eighty-five years old, said to me, "I've met all of my social obligations, and now I'm wondering what to do with the rest of my life." We talked about the CEO analogy, and after thinking about it, he said, "Why don't I, as the CEO, declare that enjoying the rest of my life is my mission and primary product?" He liked his idea, but then said mischievously, "My Vice President of Pleasure is telling me that the way to enjoy life is to go from one woman to another to another."

I laughed at the spirit of this eighty-five-year-old, still handsome and vigorous, and said, "Well, if as the CEO committed to maximizing the enjoyment in your life, you got that advice from a vice president, would you buy it?"

"Probably not," he said, but he got the point. *He* could decide.

In our stress seminar, Gail, a divorced woman in her fifties, said, "My Vice President of Appearance tells me I should get a face-lift if I want to compete socially and professionally. I'm not sure whether or not to take this advice. What do you think?"

"I think that if you were running a corporation, and one of your vice presidents suggested a direction that you weren't sure about, you'd ask for other viewpoints," I said.

She laughed heartily. "Yes, my Vice President of Finance is very opposed to the idea."

The Control Question tool can also help put aging in perspective. You don't control the passage of years. You don't control the gradual wearing down of your physical body. You don't control the fact that you will someday die. Ask yourself what you are controlling, and what it might be possible for you to control.

PATIENT FILE

from Edd Hanzelik, M.D.

YOUTHING

Even though aging is a natural part of life, my patients find it a hard pill to swallow. They view it as a failure, as if they've let themselves down by losing the full capacities they had when they were young. But one of my patients, Penelope, helped me understand that it is possible to accept and even enjoy the process.

Penelope was in her late sixties, and she had not felt well for many years. Nevertheless, she was deeply committed to getting better and was open to trying new approaches and therapies. She tried a new diet, increased her physical activity, took supplements, and began to see a therapist. Over several years, her health improved greatly. One day she told me, "This is the best I have felt in my entire life." And then she added, "I am *youthing*!"

I was quite struck by the image. I realized that "youthing" was a possibility at every stage of life. The inner qualities of youth don't just disappear as we age. We can still have curiosity, determination, enthusiasm, excitement, anticipation. There is nothing stopping us from fully engaging in life as long as we are alive.

In older people, attitude is a key to health. Time and again I have seen elderly men and women get sick after they've retired and their children have left home. The stress of thinking they no longer have purpose is too great to bear. I coach them in the understanding that they are still themselves, growing older, and that the capacity to live fully is still there. In our practice, we look at how to enjoy life to the very last breath. I love the way some patients embrace this understanding and find diverse, completely unique ways to remain vital and engaged as they live into their eighties and nineties. These efforts have a dramatically positive effect on their health and well-being.

CHOOSE YOUR TOOL

I hope you are beginning to see that no matter how challenging the circumstances, you can go to your Inner Game toolbox and find a tool that will help you overcome your stress—even when you are faced with matters of life and death. Even when you are faced with multiple stressors, you can focus on your inner stability, use your personal shield, and choose your tools to proceed with equanimity. The Inner Game can be played at a championship level, regardless of age, health, financial circumstances, or any other outer reality.

CONCLUSION
The Inner Game of Life

Someone once asked me, "How do I know if I'm playing the Inner Game well?" I answered, "It feels effortless. When you stop trying so hard, and start trusting more, success will come."

Many years ago, Jennifer Capriati, a world-class tennis player who was only fourteen years old at the time, gave an interview that has stayed with me. Observing that she was so young, a reporter noted that it must be quite scary and stressful to go up against some of the great powerhouses of the game. Jennifer replied, "If I was feeling frightened playing tennis, I don't see why I would do it."

Out of the mouths of babes! Jennifer went on to have many struggles in her life, but at that moment she was speaking as pure Self 2, without the doubts and fears imposed by Self 1, the Stress Maker. Freedom from stress happens when we allow ourselves to be present in each moment of our lives, enjoying and learning.

This is not an idealistic perspective. People have said, "Yes, in a perfect world, I would put myself first. In a perfect world, I would stop jumping when my boss said, 'Jump.' But not in the real world." But I hope you've seen, reading this book, that the more you allow the Stress Maker to dominate your thoughts and actions, the less productive you become. The less healthy you become. The less happy you become. The choice is not between being content and being successful. Being content is fundamental to success.

Playing the Inner Game well means understanding that judgments about whether you're good enough are not real. They are superimposed by others and by your own inner critic. When you're in the zone of your life, you're in the action, aware of what's happening without judging.

Think again about young children. When a child is learning to walk, he falls and gets up, falls and gets up. We don't say, "What an idiot! You can't even stand upright." No, we smile and enjoy what we recognize as a natural and beautiful process. We clap and say, "What a remarkable being!" And the child doesn't say to himself, "I'm such a klutz." No, he laughs and smiles, and tries again.

Everything about this process feels right and natural, but over time, we lose the capacity to be in the here and now, enjoying and learning. A friend who recently visited was down in the dumps. He told me, "I love my wife. I'm so happy to be married to her."

"So, why the long face?" I asked.

"Our marriage is still new," he replied. "I don't know very many people who are still happy after ten or twenty years. I'm not sure we can keep this up."

His marriage was good, but the "what-ifs" were making him miserable. How many of us allow our enjoyment of life to be spoiled by the fear of unknown catastrophes ahead?

PATIENT FILE

from John Horton, M.D.

REFLECTION AND HEALING

A new patient, Martha, a successful executive, came to talk to me about her fatigue. She already had some good medical evaluations that did not reveal any obvious physical cause for the fatigue. She had been told by a friend that I would be a good doctor to render another opinion. During the lengthy history, Martha mentioned stress a number of times as a possible cause for her fatigue, but felt that she "managed" it well with exercise, frequent mini vacations, and reasonable eating habits.

Even before the physical exam, Martha sat back in her chair and asked what I thought about her condition and stress. Because her medical condition had been well analyzed by other good doctors, I felt free to answer. The conversation that followed the question surprised both of us. It surprised me because without any explanation I invited her into an Inner Game process of discovery and reflection. We both felt the resulting insight would lift some of the burden of stress quickly.

I told Martha that she needed to understand the structure of life in order to understand stress. I asked her, "What are the necessities and priorities of your physical life?"

Martha answered, "Sleep—that's a current problem for me. Also good food, exercise, vacations."

"I think you've missed the first three priorities," I said, smiling.

She was puzzled and very interested. "What do you mean?" she asked.

"You didn't mention water," I said.

"Oh—of course."

"How about getting warm if you are very cold or cooling off if you are really hot?"

"Yes," she agreed. "That's important."

"And finally, what about air?"

Martha was amused that she had missed the top three priorities. I pointed out that the structure of our physical existence was quite clear, and that in reality the more important something is, the more simple and the more enjoyable it is. Breathing is a gift; it is so important we never even have to think about it.

Then I pointed out that the most profound causes of stress are fear and frustration. These experiences will start up the powerful currents of the fight-flight-freeze system and change our thoughts, emotions, and actions. She understood this.

I then asked her about the structure of her—and anyone's—psychological and social life. Again, we were not talking about stress, but about the structure of life. It was a spontaneous and exciting conversation for both of us.

Martha thought about it, and said social relationships are the first priority. After more reflection, she added having a good self-image. I asked if there were any other critical needs she had not mentioned. She thought and said no. I told her she had missed three, and again she was surprised and curious. I asked her if she knew about Maslow's hierarchy of needs. She did, so I pointed out that she had missed the first two needs, survival and safety. That was okay with her, because she lived in a safe place and she was wealthy.

However, when I reminded her of the need for self-actualization, she stopped and became very quiet for some time. She then said from deep conviction that she had been neglecting this need for a long time, and knew that this was the source of her fatigue.

Martha told me that she had always worked first for enjoyment, and that money and status were secondary. But over the last few months she had not been enjoying her work. We then talked about how the stress system is hardwired to feeling. Just as all those key physical needs are tied to feeling, so are the key psychological and social needs. It is a simple system based upon enjoyment. If our work or social life is not enjoyable, then we will want to leave or fight to change things or freeze (feel stuck). But our ability to rationalize is so strong that we ignore the feeling part and push ourselves to adapt. Without realizing it, Martha's stress response had been triggered by her lack of satisfaction.

The frustration of any basic need over time will lead to chronic stress reactions and possible illness. This holds true even if we are unconscious and neglectful of this need. We see patients who think they can live without love, self-esteem, or self-actualization. Until they understand these needs and work to fulfill them, they tend to remain in chronic stress and have difficulty overcoming their illness.

LETTING GO AND LIVING

I recently had the privilege of hearing the sixty-year-old adventurer Miles Hilton-Barber give a motivational talk at the end of a business management course for Rolls-Royce. His achievements included climbing Mount Kilimanjaro, the highest mountain in Africa, and Mount Blanc, the highest mountain in Western Europe. He also completed what was known as "the toughest footrace on earth"—one hundred and fifty miles across the Sahara desert in the Marathon des Sables—and crossing the entire Qatar desert nonstop in seventy-eight hours without sleep. These achievements would be remarkable for any adventurer. But Miles started these challenges when he was fifty-four and totally blind.

He said that up to that point he had been living in the prison of his blindness. At fifty, he decided not to let his blindness limit him in anything he really wanted to do. "It was this simple but profound shift in attitude that started my life as an adventurer," he explained. Not only was there wisdom in his talk, but it was delivered with the gusto of someone who believed in enjoying every single moment of his life. "It takes a lot now to cause me any stress," he said.

We have all seen examples of people who suffer unthinkable loss and move on, courageously and even joyfully. They have found ways to use their inner resources to gain stability, in spite of their pain. We admire them from afar, but we all have the ability to use our inner resources that way.

Playing the Inner Game does not mean giving up our attachments, but letting go of them when necessary. We don't want to be like the monkey who gets caught in a trap because he won't let go of an apple. Playing the Inner Game means living in the moment, but not being chained to the moment.

A woman once came to our stress seminar who didn't seem to get anything out of it. She reported being just as stressed at the end as she was at the beginning. John was curious about this, and since he knew her husband, he asked him why he thought his wife was so resistant. The man said, "She is obsessed with the lives of

our adult children. Let me put it this way. Her coffee cup has an inscription, 'If you love them, let them go. If they don't come back, hunt them down and kill them.' "

A few years later, the woman came to John as a patient, and she talked about how much trouble she was having resolving issues with her children and their families. She couldn't let go. After a few sessions, and a little time using the tools of the Inner Game, she brought the coffee cup in and handed it to John. "This is yours now," she said with a smile.

PATIENT FILE

from Edd Hanzelik, M.D.

FREE TO LOVE

Judith, a forty-eight-year-old patient, described how her first child was born with multiple congenital deformities, for which he had already had over thirty operations. I immediately felt empathy for Judith, knowing how painful this must have been for her, but her experience was different. She viewed her child's birth as the beginning of her own spiritual experience. When she attended a group for mothers of disabled children, she found it interesting that she was not reacting in the ways the other mothers were. She never blamed anyone; she never felt like a victim; she never asked "why?" Her son is now eighteen years old, attending college, and was recently selected as the Freshman Prince. She has learned a lot in the process of raising this child. When she looks at the experience, she is grateful, for it has been a very positive aspect of her life. Her story is a beautiful demonstration of how an individual can maintain stability in the face of life's challenges, and how our perception of events will determine how much stress we experience.

WHAT IS SUCCESS?

John, Edd, and I were discussing this book with our editor, who wanted to know if it would help people be successful. I've thought about that question a lot, because in my coaching I frequently ask clients to define what they mean by success. I see that most of us have been indoctrinated to think of success in a certain way. Some think success can be measured by money, power, and influence, others by a happy family life, others by standing out in their professions.

What is the meaning of success to you? Consider to what extent that meaning is shaped by society and to what extent it is your own. Take a moment to reflect on what you pursue in the name of success. Clarity about your purpose informs all the other decisions in your life. Without clarity, nothing keeps you from pursuing ends not aligned with your core desire and losing yourself in the process.

Once I was giving a presentation to corporate managers and educators. At the end of the presentation, one manager, Jim, was sobbing with his head in his hands. People started to crowd around him to comfort him and offer advice. Seeing the confusion that was resulting, I went up to Jim and asked if he'd like to take a walk. "Yes," he said in a relieved tone of voice. We walked in silence for some time before I finally asked him if he would care to say what the tears were all about. "Fear," he said. I asked him if he wanted to talk about it and at first he said, "No." We walked more in silence, and finally Jim said, "Okay, I'll tell you what my fear is. I have accomplished everything I've set my mind to in my life. My fear is that I will continue to do this all my life and then die without ever knowing who I am."

It was a stunning statement. "That's one of the noblest fears I've ever heard stated," I said. "But the fact that you have that fear also means you have the urge or desire to know who you are, and that can serve you well. If you take that need seriously it can guide you to your goal."

Jim's story makes a clear distinction between two kinds of goals, outer and inner. He felt confident that he could achieve any of the outer goals he set for himself, but was not so sure about achieving his inner goals, and this caused him great anguish.

Is there an inherent conflict between outer success and inner success? I don't think so. I've seen very wealthy people who are clearly not happy or content. I've seen poor, outwardly unsuccessful people with smiles on their faces and a look of contentment in their eyes. Likewise, there are rich people who are happy and poor people who are not. In my opinion, outer and inner success are really independent of each other. There's no reason why we cannot pursue both.

When you examine your outer goals, you discover that they are not ends in themselves. You could ask the president of the United States why he wanted to attain a certain goal. He would probably say something like, "So that I can make a difference in my country and in the world." And then if you asked him what he would attain if he achieved that, he might say, "It would give me profound satisfaction." Similarly, if you asked a wealthy man what he had hoped to gain from his wealth, he might say that ultimately he wanted to gain a sense of freedom and security. In both cases, and in many others to which you could apply the same test, you would likely discover that external success was ultimately driven by the desire for an inward state, such as happiness, contentment, security, freedom, or peace.

Outer success brings what it brings. Both the means to the goal and the goal itself can bring valuable outer and inner rewards. Inner success is assessed by inner measures. Only the individual knows if it is achieved, because it is about how one feels.

So my response to our editor was that yes, this book would help people become more successful, and possibly come to their own inner definition of success.

THE GIFT

I feel sad when I reflect on the times in my life when I haven't been able to accept myself as I am. Sometimes the failure has been my tendency to lean toward what might be called the dark side. At other times it's been my unwillingness to accept the beautiful side. In my early conditioning it was perfectly okay to admit shortcomings. But to acknowledge, especially publicly, the part of myself I liked and respected—that was a no-no. I was taught that stating what was beautiful, what was gifted, what was truly individual about me would be egotistical and bragging. The cost of this concept was that I became more familiar with the negative side than the positive, and I was constantly burdened with changing one into the other. The bad must become good, the weak strong, the incompetent competent, the boring charming. I was surrounded by idealism and thought the purpose of life was to measure up to the ideals I or someone else invented. Frankly, the game is very stressful. It doesn't feel good, and after a while it gets boring and tiresome.

I've found that the only way out of this game is to dig deep beneath all of the idealism and discover who I am. When I'm caught up in the "trying to change myself" game, it's hard to see that I'm already beautiful. It makes me sigh with relief when I realize that I was beautiful as a young child, just as all young children are. Beneath the idealism, I have found a natural thirst—to know, to appreciate, to admire, to enjoy. It comes to me as an innate desire, unlike the ideals I've bought into. It's a desire to know who I already am and have always been. It's a desire to accept the possibilities I have as a human being. It's not a game. It's real. It's grounded in fact. I am alive. I am breathing. And I want to be free of the games people play in the arenas of public opinion. I want a relationship with the self I am, as I was created. I want to remember that this gift of life is limited, and I want to make the most of the time I am given.

Something in me says, "Well that's nothing special—everyone is alive and breathing. What's the big deal?" But then, in quiet moments, I realize that it *is* a big deal—a very big deal for me and for everyone. I'm not here to compete with others, but to discover and explore what the big deal is about being here at all. What the big deal is about breathing. What the big deal is about being able to love, being glad to be alive, being grateful, and quite simply, enjoying.

When I was a young child, I frequently thought about what it was going to be like when I died. My imagination took me to a place where God would be saying to me something like: "Well, Tim, you're back. Let's see, we put you on earth in 1938 in San Francisco, second son in an upper-middle-class family. You had the best education and many talents and opportunities. And in your lifetime the world was full of terrible problems." Then came the big question, "So what did you do about it?" I always felt worried that I'd fall short.

It wasn't until my thirties that my imagination took me on a different journey. No pearly gates, no angels, just God and a representative talking to each other with me present. God was saying, "How long did we spend making this planet, Earth—several billion years, wasn't it? And how long did it take for us to evolve the human body? Millions and millions of years, as I remember. We put a lot into it." Then, looking at me, God said, "We gave you one of those human bodies. Not a bat, or a worm, or a hippopotamus, but a top-of-the-line body to live life on a top-of-the-line planet with other human beings." Then came a new big question: "So, how did you like it? And what did you like most?"

I saw myself replying, "How did I like it? I really didn't have time to enjoy it that much. I was too busy fixing the world and fixing myself to merely enjoy it."

Imagining this conversation, I thought, "What a pity." I missed the whole point of the gift. Of course, any giver wants to know if you liked the gift you were given, and if you'd even unwrapped the package.

Ultimately, the Inner Game is about unwrapping and enjoying the gift of life. At times it might seem difficult, but it's actually the most natural thing in the world. At the moment we were born, we were gifted with wonderful potentials for consciousness, joy, peace, freedom, and countless other abilities. To see us use and delight in these gifts is all any giver could ask for.

APPENDIX A

MEDICAL NOTES

QUESTIONS AND ANSWERS ABOUT STRESS, THE BRAIN, AND HEALTH

*John Horton, M.D.,
and Edward Hanzelik, M.D.*

What happens in the body when we experience stress?

The brain perceives a threat and alerts the amygdala or the hippocampus, which along with the hypothalamus arouses the sympathetic nervous system, the pituitary gland, and the adrenal glands (located on top of the kidneys). The net effect is the production of the basic stress hormones, adrenaline and cortisone.

As a result of this hormonal activity, the heart rate and blood pressure increase. Blood rushes preferentially to the muscles. This is all in preparation for fight or flight. If there is a freeze reaction, the opposite occurs: both blood pressure and heart rate decrease.

The digestive system also gets into the act. The body understands that in a life-or-death situation there is no time to digest food. So the digestive process is turned off by reducing blood flow and decreasing digestive enzymes and saliva. The immune system contracts and becomes less active. The sexual and reproductive functions also diminish during periods of chronic stress.

The body is very smart. It knows what to do in response to a temporary crisis. But this systemic activity is supposed to be very short-lived. If the stress response continues and becomes chronic, the formerly protective activities become damaging.

How do I know if I am being affected by stress?

Most people can feel when they are under stress. They see situations that are difficult for them and for which they do not have easy solutions. They can feel the ways in which their bodies are affected by the state of uncertainty they are experiencing.

The stress system is activated automatically, without choice. For example, if you are in a stressful situation such as sitting in the examination room waiting for your doctor to come in, you may notice your heart is beating a little more rapidly, your breathing is a little faster, and you are perspiring, especially in your armpits. Why? In anticipation of the possible threat of what your doctor will say or do, stress hormones are being released, and you are getting ready to fight or run. The body, anticipating that you will produce a lot of heat while fighting or running, is already producing sweat to cool you down.

Why does stress feel bad?

Your brain unconsciously interprets many simple situations as threats to your existence—such as a disagreement with a spouse, a misbehaving child, a nonfunctioning piece of equipment, a time commitment, even thoughts about yourself or anything else. All of these stressors can initiate the same stress response that animals depend on to survive life-threatening attacks. Humans usually don't fight or run, so the chronic activation of the stress system leads to an accumulation of the stress hormones, which causes the basic function of health maintenance to be placed on hold. The immune, digestive, reproductive, and hormonal systems are all turned down as the body gears up to fight for its life.

You can imagine that a chemical imbalance of this degree will feel bad and bring on many symptoms. Because of the discomfort, people will try to feel better by using substances such as cigarettes, alcohol, caffeine, food, sugar, and prescription and recreational drugs, which, of course, only makes matters worse.

According to Phil W. Gold, M.D., the former chief of psycho-neuro-endocrinology at the National Institute of Mental Health (NIMH), the stress system is hardwired to feeling. Threat, frustration of needs, and pain provoke this system. We may ignore bad feelings because we do not see a way out of the stress, or because we have been taught to "suck it up." We may have rationalizations for why we should ignore the discomfort. Unfortunately, as long as we feel bad and the stress system is up-regulated, we will experience physical, mental, emotional, and social consequences.

What are the symptoms of chronic stress?

Chronic stress can affect any aspect of the body. Common symptoms include tense muscles, especially at the base of the neck, digestive disturbances, headaches, menstrual irregularity, palpitations, chest pain, irritability, decreased sexual performance, impaired thinking, skin rashes, sleep disturbances, and fatigue. Stress can also make any underlying condition worse, including diabetes, hypertension, arthritis, infections, and many more. Also, people experiencing stress have a tendency to neglect care of themselves, which also intensifies these symptoms.

But don't we need the fight-flight-freeze reaction to survive? Isn't stress good sometimes?

For the most part, we are not talking about truly life-threatening situations as catalysts for the stress response in humans. Most of our worst fear, frustration, and pain is evoked by the internal Stress Maker, and fleeing, fighting, and freezing do not help.

A. T. Simeons, a student of the stress pioneer Hans Selye, wrote in 1961, "Fight-flight is an antiquated mechanism that has not kept evolutionary pace with the development of the human mind." Of course, the stress system has its place. If you are engaged freely in a challenging activity, such as skiing down a slope or giving a public talk, your stress system will activate and help gear you up for the challenge. Your vision and thinking will become clearer. Your body will be prepared for the coming demand. Or if you are in a genuinely life-threatening situation, such as a fire in your home, the stress system will quickly mobilize your resources to save your life. These are situations in which stress is good, but they are a very small percentage of the stressors we encounter. As soon as stress becomes chronic and persistent, the biochemical imbalance created interferes with health, performance, and mental clarity.

Can stress lead to illness?

Stress clearly opens the door to many illnesses, but no single disease has been proven to be caused solely by stress. The direct effects of the stress system—to raise the pulse, blood pressure, and blood sugar—can bring on or worsen hypertension, diabetes, arrhythmias, and heart conditions in susceptible people. Cortisone antagonizes insulin, which worsens the metabolic syndrome, leading to weight gain, high cholesterol, and heart disease. Many digestive diseases can be triggered by stress, including irritable bowel syndrome, colitis, ulcers, and acid reflux. The suppression of the immune system by stress makes you more susceptible to infections, even the common cold, and interferes with normal healing.

Over time, with the fatiguing of the adrenals, the immune system can become overactive and lead to allergies or autoimmune diseases, such as lupus and rheumatoid arthritis. The impact on the bone worsens osteoporosis and delays growth in children. Chronic fatigue and fibromyalgia are both exacerbated by stress, as are respiratory problems such as asthma. Psychologic disorders, including depression, anxiety, obsessive-compulsive disorder, and alcoholism are all greatly influenced by stress. Chronic stress clearly distorts the normal functioning and balance of the body systems.

If I decrease my stress, will that improve my health or cure illnesses?

Decreasing stress does improve health. Illnesses are easier to treat. Since illnesses generally have other roots besides stress, relieving the stress alone may not cure most of them, but will help to bring about the cure. We turn to specific activities to improve our health and prevent disease, including better nutrition, exercise, good sleep, avoiding harmful substances, and regular medical checkups. In our experience, reducing and avoiding stress will affect each of these factors, and it is as important as any of them in avoiding disease and promoting health.

What scientific evidence supports the Inner Game approach?

The field of neurobiology is helping to provide a more in-depth understanding of the human brain and the mind. The functions of the middle prefrontal cortex of the brain, described by Daniel Siegel in *The Mindful Brain*, include bodily regulation (balancing the sympathetic and parasympathetic nervous systems), attuned communication (coordinating input from your mind with another's), emotional balance, response flexibility (the ability to pause before action—the root of the STOP tool), empathy (the root of the Transpose tool), insight (self-knowing awareness), fear modulation, intuition (processing deep ways of knowing), and morality (what is best for the whole and not just for oneself).

These brain centers have been observed to maintain their ability to grow until the very end of life. The Inner Game focuses on the many built-in resources we have as hardware and offers tools to increase access to them. Scientific studies are confirming the existence of these resources, as well as our ability to enhance our access to them.

Can inner resources overcome stress?

There has been a great deal of interesting research that shows the necessity of love—one of the primary inner resources. Rene Spitz, a French pediatrician, made an important observation when he was called to consult at an orphanage in France at the end of World War II where children were dying in the first year of life. The orphanage wanted Dr. Spitz to find the infectious agent that was causing the deaths, but he could not find one. In fact, the hygiene of the infants was good. However, Dr. Spitz did notice that none of the children were being held and played with by any of the caretakers. Everything was task-oriented. When Dr. Spitz asked the caretakers to express love and play with the infants, the deaths stopped occurring.

Harry Harlow, a psychologist in the United States, did an experiment which confirmed Rene Spitz's observations. He raised monkeys with either real mothers or cloth mothers. The cloth mothers were designed to be exactly the size of monkeys. They had wire bodies with cloth covering them, and bottles where the breasts would be so that the infant monkeys could be fed as they were from their mother. The monkeys "raised" by cloth mothers couldn't socialize, and they exhibited many behavioral problems. The monkeys raised by real mothers socialized normally.

Recently, at the National Institutes of Health, a study was conducted with Rhesus monkeys showing that anxious mothers produced anxious children who did not integrate well into the monkey tribe. In order to discover whether this was caused by genetics or nurturing, the researchers removed some of the young monkeys and gave them to mothers who were not anxious. They grew up to be nonanxious adults. Animal rights activists have protested these studies, asserting that the findings were obvious.

Norman Cousins described in *Anatomy of an Illness* the great potential of another inner resource, humor. Faced with a life-threatening illness, he watched hilarious movies, laughing raucously thoughout the day. Remarkably, with this and other natural treatments, he recovered from the illness and was asked to be an Adjunct Professor of Medical Humanities at UCLA Medical School to teach about his experience.

When you think about the different nervous systems, it makes a lot of sense that when children grow up with a great deal of stress—particularly with abusive violence, anger, emotional distance, or neglect—the more primitive parts of their brains will dominate their responses. When children grow up in loving, laughing, and nurturing environments, there is a much better chance for their nervous systems to develop in a healthier way. There are four things children need for healthy nervous systems: basic physical care and protection, to be enjoyed and appreciated, genuine love, and to be understood as unique beings. Wouldn't there be a lot less crime, substance abuse, and mental illness if each child received these four basic needs from the adults and cultures who care for them?

What is the role of hope, another of the inner resources?

"Hope is one of our central emotions, but we are often at a loss when asked to define it," writes Jerome Groopman in his recent book, *The Anatomy of Hope*. "Many of us confuse hope with optimism, a prevailing attitude that 'things turn out for the best.' But hope differs from optimism. Hope does not arise from being told to 'think positively,' or from hearing an overly rosy forecast. Hope, unlike optimism, is rooted in unalloyed reality." In our experience, all of the inner resources are rooted in unalloyed reality.

What about Post-Traumatic Stress Disorder?

Often, traumatic or stressful experiences from childhood are a hidden source of stress in adults. Because the memory is so painful, or because the experience happened at such a young age, it is often repressed from conscious memory.

The biology of PTSD is different from chronic stress. The hormone of severe stress is adrenaline. It works quickly to mobilize our bodies for extreme reactions to serious threat. Adrenaline reactions are uncomfortable and require action to resolve the situation. The hormone of chronic stress is cortisol, also made by the adrenal gland. It mobilizes the body's resources for the long haul of stress. Some of the most common stress-related illnesses, such as depression and metabolic syndrome, are associated with high cortisol levels.

It may be that in PTSD the adrenaline reaction continues and the cortisol reaction is absent or not able to overcome the sense of immediate threat. We know that in PTSD, adrenaline reactions can be triggered by events that remind the person of the initial traumatic event or events, such as a loud noise for a combat survivor or an aggressive male stranger for a rape survivor. In the case of early childhood trauma, sometimes the triggers are obscure but nevertheless create serious reactions.

Part of the mechanism of PTSD is the firing of the amygdala, which kindles many reactive pathways in our thinking brains. We cannot influence this kindling by thinking because it happens too quickly and we have no control over the amygdala from our thinking brains.

Treating PTSD is notoriously difficult. Dr. Horton, after seeing a number of people afflicted with PTSD in his practice, developed a workshop focused on the natural healing of emotional wounds.

The workshop sought to look at potential remedies for these experiences. Dr. Horton asked participants to put each possible remedy into one of three boxes: one for things which were always helpful to anyone; the second for things that were not helpful and could be harmful; and the third for things that were relative—they could be helpful or harmful depending on the person and the circumstances. The groups identified five things that they felt were always healing to everyone: love, self-understanding, a commitment to get better, hope, and the acceptance of life's gifts. This conclusion is consistent with the Inner Game approach. The notion that we have inherent resources that cannot be disturbed or destroyed by trauma is true and gives hope.

A major redefining process is involved in resolving PTSD. Healing begins with an understanding and acceptance that the stress reactions are triggered by associations with events in the past that cannot be changed. The reactions are separate from the self. With this clarity, the inner resources can become good friends, and life experience can shift to learning and enjoyment.

What if stress from the past has left a lasting effect on the body?

Stress from childhood can change the structure of the brain, so the amygdala is more likely to respond to stressors. We see many people whose nervous systems have been up-regulated by stress. Their bodies often have symptoms that have accumulated from years of increased stress. The tools of the Inner Game can help begin the process of relieving the body of the past harmful effects of stress.

Many other approaches are also helpful, including massage, traditional Chinese medicine with acupuncture, nutritional supplements, meditation, exercise, yoga, psychotherapy, and medications. Dr. Herbert Benson wrote about the Relaxation Response, an innate tendency of the body to unwind, brought on by simple meditation techniques. When individuals utilize the best of modern medicine, and integrative medicine, and combine them with their best self-care, amazing results are possible. Individual learning is key, because every person is unique. One size does not fit all.

Also, in childhood we learn from so-called mirror neurons—that is, we mirror or copy what we see in our family and culture. We may also mirror or copy the inner emotions and thoughts of those that influence us. The new medical models of psychological change focus on neuronal plasticity, which allows the growth of new circuitry anytime in life. Neuronal plasticity allows for the growth of fresh circuits that transcend past experiences.

Do men and women react the same to stress?

Recent studies suggest that males and females of various species react differently to stress. Instead of fight or flight, the response of females has been described as "tend and befriend." This is seen as an evolutionary response by females to protect themselves, using their strengths of working together and caring for others.

The perception of stressors can often also be different between males and females, with women more aware of the subtler stressors of human communication and feelings. Another difference is that women may focus on the details of the situation when stressed, while men tend to take a larger or more philosophical view. This can cause conflict between men and women, the men thinking the women are lost in details and unable to see the "big picture," the women seeing the men as impractical and lost in thought.

The Inner Game is common ground for both sexes. We have the same inherent abilities and the same inner pathways of wisdom to develop. In our workshops we see both men and women shift their focus from the external aspects of stress to the Inner Game, with an enhanced ability to build stability and avoid loss of balance.

We hope you have seen that, when it comes to stress, you have a choice. You can accept the automatic activation of the stress system, or you can make the effort to respond from inner clarity and wisdom. Each of us has all the qualities we need to have the inner stability that allows us to maintain our balance in the face of life's challenges. We know that being defined and driven by the stress response will open the doors to illness, poor performance, and unhappiness. But we also know that learning to outsmart life's challenges and build our stability can help us fulfill our potential and truly enjoy our existence.

APPENDIX B

INNER GAME RESOURCES

To learn more about the Inner Game, go to Tim Gallwey's website at *www.theinnergame.com.*

The Inner Game of Stress continues Gallwey's Inner Game series. Other titles include:

The Inner Game of Golf (Random House)—revised 2009 edition.

The Inner Game of Tennis (Random House trade)—revised 1997 edition.

The Inner Game of Work (Random House)—1999.

Inner Skiing (Random House)—revised 1997 edition.

The Inner Game of Music with Barry Green (Random House)—1986.

FURTHER READING

We recommend the following titles for those who want to increase their understanding of stress and the human potential to overcome it:

Benson, H. (1975). *The Relaxation Response.* NY, NY: Morrow

Cannon, W. B. (1932) (revised 1939). *The Wisdom of the Body.* NY, NY: Norton

Eliot, R. S. & Breo, D. L. (1984). *Is It Worth Dying For?* NY, NY: Bantam

Epictetus (1994) (New Interpretation by Sharon Lebell). *The Art of Living.* SF, CA: HarperCollins

Groopman, J. (2004). *The Anatomy of Hope.* NY, NY: Random House

Kabat-Zinn, Jon (1990). *Full Catastrophe Living.* NY, NY: Delacorte Press

Lehrer, P. M., Woolfolk, R. L. & Sime, W. E. (Eds.) (2007). *Principles and Practice of Stress Management (3rd Ed.).* NY, NY: Guilford Press

Sapolsky, R. M. (1998). *Why Zebras Don't Get Ulcers.* NY, NY: Barnes & Noble

Seaward, B. L. (2002). *Managing Stress.* Sudbury, MA: Jones and Bartlett

Selye, H. (1956, 1984). *The Stress of Life (2nd Ed.).* NY, NY: McGraw-Hill

Siegel, D. J. (2007). *The Mindful Brain.* NY, NY: Norton

Siegel, D. J. (1999). *The Developing Brain.* NY, NY: Guilford Press

ACKNOWLEDGMENTS

We are thankful for the tremendous support of many people in the creation of this work. In particular to

Catherine Whitney: who took the passion and insights of the three of us and crafted them into a book we are all proud of.

Jane Dystel: our agent, who believed in this book and patiently encouraged us to create it.

Mark Tavani: our editor from Random House, who embraced the work with passion and insight, and stewarded its development.

Joan Swan: whose creative illustrations capture the spirit of our writing.

Individually, we are grateful for the many people who have supported our lives and work.

Tim Gallwey

Special thanks to

Irene Gallwey—my older sister, for her encouragement, feedback, and love.

Mary Wishard—my younger sister, for her encouragement, feedback, and love.

Zach Kleiman—for his special coaching on and off the tennis court.

Valerio Pascotto—for his special contribution to the book, and for his enduring friendship and partnership.

Sean Brawley—my friend, for his support and enthusiasm for this book and for all aspects of the Inner Game.

Leslye Deitch—for her efforts to make this book all it could be.

Joe Fox—my first editor at Random House, for his belief in the Inner Game.

John Horton and Edd Hanzelik—my co-authors, for their dedication to this team project and their profound impact on my understanding of stability and stress.

Muriel Servais—my dear friend, for her enduring support and accurate feedback.

Michael Bolger—my friend and advisor on all things financial.

Pete Carroll—for his respect for the Inner Game and his commitment to apply it to football and to life.

Virginie Garro—whose coaching and friendship helped me through rough spots.

Edd Hanzelik, M.D.

My special thanks and gratitude go to

My dear family members, whose love and kindness fills my life, and who consistently support my evolution as an individual, as a doctor, and as an author: My dear wife, Lynne; my children, Richard and Catharine; my brother and sister, Carl and Naomi; my grandchildren, Jessica and Austin; and my great-granddaughter, Liliana.

Prem Rawat, a wonderful friend who has helped me realize the possibilities in my life, and has inspired me to discover and deepen my own inner stability.

My co-authors, Tim Gallwey and John Horton, from whom I have learned so much and with whom it has been a pleasure to create this possibility of reducing people's stress.

My colleagues and staff, who are good friends and who contribute so much to making my practice of medicine a joy, including: Anil Daya, Jane McGuire, Judy Pickering, Terry Yingling, Pratibha Kumar, Henry Warszawski, and all the others.

The sources of my education at Columbia College, Albert Einstein College of Medicine, and Beth Israel Hospital in Boston, which always balanced the wise understanding of medical knowledge with the heartfelt care of individuals. In particular, I am thankful for the inspiring example set by my chief of medicine, Dr. Howard Hiatt.

The researchers and writers who established the nature of stress and its impact on human functioning, including Hans Selye, Walter Cannon, Robert Sapolsky, John Kabat-Zinn, and many others.

The pioneers of integrative medicine, many of whom I first met in the 1970s at the American Holistic Medical Association, who courageously lead the effort to transform the way medicine is practiced. In particular, I acknowledge the work of Andrew Weil, Patch Adams, Bernie Siegel, Jeffrey Bland, Christiane Northrup, and Deepak Chopra.

And my dear patients and friends, who invite me into their lives and help me understand the art of living. Thank you all!

John Horton, M.D.

My thanks goes to

The peoples of Lesotho and India, who showed me as a young student the possibility of inner joy.

My teachers at Columbia College, in the department of Asian Studies, who helped me understand the rich possibilities for an inner life of wisdom and contentment—especially Donald Keene, William DeBary, and Chiang Yee.

My professors at Duke Medical School, who showed me the art of medicine and inspired me to understand the mind and body in diagnosing and treating illness—especially Sandy Cohen, Eugene Stead, Mort Bogdanoff, Fred Hines, Bernie Bressler, Hans Lowenbach, and Edward Busse.

My close friends and colleagues, James Ballenger, M.D., and Phil Gold, M.D., who have shared their discoveries about stress and their wonderful lives and families for over four decades.

My co-writer, medical partner, and friend, Edd Hanzelik, who hung in there with me through thick and thin for many years, and who inspires me with his extraordinary dedication and sincerity.

Tim Gallwey, a gifted, wonderful, loyal friend, who also has created the Inner Game that benefits so many people. He has been the calm rock in creating this book.

My current clinical group and colleagues, especially Anil Daya, Henry Warszawski, Pratibha Kumar, Jane Rollins, Jane McGuire, Judy Pickering, Terry Yingling, Claire Douglas, Gail Devlin and Darlene Plant.

Dr. Dan Siegel, for his writing and seminars that showed me the basis of the inner game in modern neurobiology.